THE DYNAMISM
OF SPACE

THE
DYNAMISM
OF
SPACE

A Theological Study into
the Nature of Space

IAIN M. MacKENZIE
Canon Residentiary of Worcester

The Canterbury Press
Norwich

© Iain M. MacKenzie 1995

First published 1995 by The Canterbury Press Norwich
(a publishing imprint of Hymns Ancient & Modern Limited
a registered charity)
St Mary's Works, St Mary's Plain,
Norwich, Norfolk, NR3 3BH

Iain MacKenzie has asserted his right under the Copyright, Designs
and Patents Act, 1988, to be identified as Author of this Work

British Library Cataloguing in Publication Data

A catalogue record for this book is available
from the British Library

ISBN 1–85311–117–1

*Typeset by Waveney Studios,
Diss, Norfolk
Printed and bound in Great Britain by
Anthony Rowe Ltd
Chippenham, Wiltshire*

For Bishop David Jenkins and Professor Thomas Torrance for whose generous tutelage I am grateful, having benefited by the fact that: λαμπάδια ἔχοντες διαδώσουσιν ἀλλήλοις [Plato]

Contents

Acknowledgements

Time and space are inseparable; neither can be treated in isolation from the other. They are the two-fold description we use to indicate the nature of this created existence and context which is ours – the days and places of our being. It was necessary that in writing with the emphasis on *time* in *The Anachronism of Time*, I should follow that book with a work particularly on *space*. In the first book, space could not be ignored; neither can time in this subsequent work.

I am grateful to the many people and to those reviewers who read *The Anachronism of Time* as it was intended to be treated – not as a book of conclusions, but as a work laying out the problems connected with thinking about time and as a spur for others to think further on the subject. Their encouragement and comments have been most helpful. I trust that this present work will be perceived also to be an encouragement to others to think about space theologically; it is only part of a continuing process of thought which requires contributions other than mine. I equally trust that it will be received accordingly. Statements abound in both books. They are not to be construed as conclusions, but as pointers, or even goads, directing to the fulness of the wonder of creation as a matter of God's grace, corresponding in its created rationality to that Uncreated Rationality which He is. That fulness, of course, will only be grasped when we no longer see in part and understand in part, but are face to face with the Father and Creator of all when that which is perfect is come.

I already have made full acknowledgement in *The Anachronism of Time* to my tutors and benefactors. To two of these this book is dedicated by way of thanks – Tom Torrance and David Jenkins. I am indebted to them.

For suggestions and encouragement from practitioners in other disciplines, I owe much to Dr Jonathan Rawlings,

Lecturer in Astrophysics at University College, London, and, in historical studies, to Mr Giles Gasper of Christ Church, Oxford, for his constant support and observations from his particular field. In the arduous task of correcting typescript, my thanks are due to Mrs Winifred Young, Worcester Cathedral, and in the equally taxing work of revising the proofs, to Mr Christopher Guy, the Cathedral Archaeologist. My wife and children have been most understanding about my disappearances into the study to pursue this work, whenever the duties of a Residentiary Canon would allow. My thanks are to them in abundant measure.

I am again indebted to Mr Kenneth Baker and his colleagues of The Canterbury Press Norwich for the help and kindness which I have experienced throughout the preparation and finishing of this book.

Permission to quote from the published works noted in the Select Bibliography has been generously given by Oxford University Press, the British Academy, T. and T. Clark, and Darton, Longman and Todd. For facilitating these permissions, I am grateful to Auriol Milford of O.U.P., Janet English of The British Academy, Dr Geoffrey Green of T. and T. Clark, and Morag Reeve of D.L.T. Extracts from the Authorized Version of the Bible (The King James Bible), the rights of which are vested in the Crown, are reproduced by permission of the Crown's Patentee, Cambridge University Press. For expediting this last permission, I am grateful to Linda Nicol, of C.U.P.

It should be noted that when the word 'man' is used in this book, this is to be construed inclusively and as in keeping with the original texts used.

Iain MacKenzie, Easter, 1995

Prologue

'A COMPANY of angels can dance on the point of a needle'. This saying, with variations, has been attributed falsely to St Thomas Aquinas. He never said so in these words. Certainly in his *Summa Theologiae* the subject of angels and their relation to space and time is examined at some length, intricacy and ingenuity[1].

The supposed quotation, and others similar, is levelled at what is seen to be the absurd waste of time and the intellectual vanity and triviality of the Middle Ages. This attitude of disdain has an aura about it of the self-ascribed superiority of that episode curiously called the 'Enlightenment'.

The statement about angels and needles is sometimes cited even now as having come from the mental activity of mediaeval fancies. Certainly the author has heard it twice from the pulpit[2], and this by some regarded as 'acclaimed' preachers, neither of whom were concerned with any logical argument but with the subjective, emotional fervour of the heart being 'spirit-filled', and of both of whom even the Enlightenment would have washed its hands for their vacuity of mind. All of which merely underlines the anti-intellectualism which presently pervades certainly the Church of England and, no doubt, other churches too. Such scorn is to be expected from those who have neither the will nor the ability to even think about the issues which Aquinas and others were addressing. But equally the dismissal by supposed intellects of 'mediaeval preoccupations' is also to be rejected. The superiority so exhibited comes under the stricture[3] *Let not the conceit of intellect hinder thee from worshipping mystery.*

The theologians of the Middle Ages were, in their supposed mental contortions and fancies, wrestling with a profound question. For behind their angelology lay the problem which they had the courage to tackle – the relation of what they perceived to be eternity and infinity to the material creation with its spatial and temporal constrictions and measure. That they sometimes chose angelology as the vehicle for the conveyance of their thoughts on the matter was because that was the legacy which they had inherited from the early church – particularly through the writings of Pseudo-Dionysius, which, of eastern Christian origin, possibly of the late 5th century, had, by that time, gained much vogue and circulation in the west, particularly in the issue of celestial hierarchies and created orders.

Coupled with this were the influences of Augustine of Hippo, and of the Neo-Platonic forms of thought which accompanied the wake of that 4th century western father of the Church. The observations on light, on angels and their place in creation, by the Islamic commentators, to whom the church of the early Middle Ages in the west appealed for its sources on much of its speculations and strugglings with the doctrine of creation, also had their colour with which Christian theological endeavour was tinted.

Angelology also concentrated the mystery of such a relation on the question of light, for angels were perceived to be the first creatures, born from the purest created light, and nearest to, and attendant on, the Uncreated Light which God is. In their activity towards the dimmer light of humanity, they brought to bear on the mind that question of the nature of light and its significance for creation as a creation of space and time.

Light most certainly had a dominant part in many of the mediaeval writers on the subject of creation. They appreciated the two-fold nature of light: to let be seen the entities and realities of creation, and, in that illuminating function, to enlighten the mind, that these entities and realities might be interpreted. Here, too, the function of angels as the messengers from the realms of pure light was not without place in mediaeval thought.

But of light as light in its relation to all creation and to the Creator, the significant works of John Philoponos, the 6th century Alexandrian thinker, who may be regarded as a theologian of light, must have had their part in western thought. Although his works were known to some of the

Islamic commentators, and doubtless his influence passed via their works in turn into the west, I cannot but feel that his works, even if the authorship were unknown or unacknowledged, lie, either first or second hand, in books of patristic proof texts (where authorship was not necessarily noted) such as Defensor's *Liber Scintillarum, The Book of Shining Lights*. Such books had wide circulation in the west. Philoponos's significance lies in his analysis of light as that which relates Creator and creation, the Creator being Uncreated Light and the author and upholder of created light, the characteristic of all that is.

There are many parallels in thought between Philoponos and Robert Grosseteste, particularly in the latter's *Hexaemeron* and in his small but immensely important treatise *De Luce*. This represents perhaps the climax of mediaeval thought on the subject of light and creation and its relation to the Creator.

But the whole subject of the nature of creation and to what it may be related ultimately is one which preoccupied many minds in that period, even if later unthinking detractors of its efforts, preoccupied with thoughts of their own developed superior ways of thought, scoffed at the attempts of some of their earlier fellows to think the problem through via such motifs as angelology. In so doing they missed the real seriousness of the earlier endeavour, and, parcelling all mediaeval thinkers together, passed by in ignorance the great contribution of such as Grosseteste to the slowing down of the advance of true rational expression through the perception of the fundamental questions concerning creation.

The whole question of the nature of the universe and to what it may be ultimately related is an inter-disciplinary one, shared by science, theology, mathematics and philosophy. This book is an attempt, from the standpoint of systematic theology, to contribute to that debate (which hopefully is a conversation) concentrating on the question of the nature of space.

I already have tried to make some contribution to this in my previous work *The Anachronism of Time*, but, fully aware that time and space are inseparably bound, now try to view the question more from the aspect of a consideration of the nature of space as far as the theologian is concerned.

What is space? As with that same question about time, everyone assumes that they know the answer until they pause and really think. Time, it may be, as the most common concept of it arises in the mind, is described as a measurement. But 'a measurement of what?' is the next stage in the questioning as to what time is. For it is not the measurement which is time, for the measurement is but a convenience.

Likewise with space. The first thing which comes into mind perhaps is the 'far reaches of space', a sense of directional magnitude. But that again is a measurement judgment of the mind, however imprecise. It does not answer the question or even touch the problem.

These questions about time and space are, at the fundamental level of looking at the problem, asked from the wrong premises. It is assumed that the question, at root, is one of quantity, whereas it is really directed to quality. But we circumvent that difficulty by transferring it into the realms of quantity – because we feel we have the capability of quantifying and mastering measurement. Even the concept of 'infinity' can become such an illusion, at least to the extent that its introduction into an answer to the question shows that we have grasped the problem.

The dilemma of time as treated as a measurement lies in the definition of the 'present'. This defies recordable measurement and confounds any attempt to answer it out of quantifiable concepts. Indeed, the whole convenience of describing time as 'past', 'present' and 'future', is shown to be a mere convenience when the challenge is given to quantify the past and the future, let alone the present. The argument I have outlined about this dilemma in *The Anachronism of Time* has a parallel in the whole idea of space.

As with time, where the dilemma centres on the 'present' and what that is, so with space, where the fundamental question, I am sure, should be 'what is place?' What makes 'place' place?

It would not appear initially that this is a very helpful conjecture. The child's questioning – 'where is God?', 'where is heaven?' – would seem to indicate that a consideration of place is not an advantageous entrance into the question of space, such is the racking of parents' brains to give a satisfactory answer without disappointing the child or advocating a disappointing (not to say disappointed) God. It merely seems to confound the issue. Yet it is not really a question about place. It is a question about God.

When more mature (though thereby not more serious) questions are asked about place – 'what is place?', it is significant that invariably the answers come in one aesthetic form or another. Place is generally described in terms of quality, rather than quantity. Yet place and space are inseparable.

Let me put forward an initial thought as an entrance into the appreciation of what the question really is and the direction, therefore, in which the answer is to be sought; and this is that *place is significant space*.

By this I mean several things developing in sequence.

First, that it is identifiable space. Second, that the identity does not depend on measurement. Third, that the identity does depend on events. Fourth, that these events are the expression of existence or existences. Fifth, place is the space or room which these existences make for themselves and determine by their presence and activity. Sixth, place is therefore that which is qualified by the nature of the existences and their activities. Seventh, that place is quantified is only secondary and tenuous on that quality if it is possible at all. Eighth, if it is quantifiable, it is so only in terms of where the activities and existences peculiar to one thing or sets of things either cease or give way to other existences of things in their particular and differing activities. Ninth, place is to be described dynamically therefore. Tenth, measurement is static if treated as the primary way to define place and leads to a false appreciation of what place is.

But in saying that *place is significant space*, I do not mean to imply that there is space which is insignificant. Again, our lamentable tendency to quantify everything as the prerequisite for our understanding of it, tends to lead us into descriptions such as 'empty' space, or 'nothingness' – meaning by the latter some concept such as a vacuum or the void stretching on and on, even endlessly or infinitely. Here we still have not rid ourselves of the preoccupation with measurement, even if we acknowledge in the use of the word 'infinite' our ultimate inability to cope with it.

What I do mean is that place is essentially a particular existence making room for itself in its own activity, and that space is perhaps to be perceived as the sum total of such existences and activities in their relation and interaction one with another.

We will be dealing with the term 'infinity' in later chapters. All I wish to do is to sow a doubt, namely: that the concept, tantalising as it may be, can become a red herring if it is allowed to be the primary issue with regard to the nature of space. There are many questions hovering which have to be addressed. They are summed up in the question: is infinity a mathematical or an ontological concept? That is, is it a mathematical theory with no substance in reality, or is it an *attempt* to describe the nature of what is called space as this space is supposed to exist?

We will have recourse to this distinction later. Let Locke (who despite his Enlightenment label did make one or two sensible observations, even if, as in this case, his general modus philosophiae contradicted them) provoke thought here[4]:

> I have been hitherto apt to think that the great and inextricable difficulties which perpetually involve all discourses concerning infinity, whether of space, duration or divisibility, have been the certain marks of a defect in our ideas of infinity, and the disproportion the nature thereof has to the comprehension of our narrow capacities. For, whilst men talk and dispute of infinite space or duration, as if they had as complete and positive ideas of them as they have of the names they use for them, or as they have of a yard, or an hour, or any other determinative quantity, it is no wonder if the incomprehensible nature of the thing they discourse of, or reason about, leads them into perplexities and contradictions, and their minds be overlaid by an object too large and mighty to be surveyed and managed by them.

Locke highlights two errors: that our ideas of infinity are questionable: and that we assume that our minds have the capacity to deal with the infinite. In all that follows in this work, these two questioning strictures should be seen to be hanging, Damoclean-like, over the outlining and discussion of how infinity has been and is being dealt with as a concept.

It is unfortunate that Locke's attitude of mind was pervaded by the influence of Isaac Newton, with the latter's categories of absolute time and absolute space as a framework into which everything which exists was fitted and within which reality was interpreted. But here at least there is an open statement which goes as far as disparaging the arrogance which seeks to dissect and analyse the problem of infinity and has the temerity to think that it is solvable.

We may wish to question not just those who think so highly of their mental capacities, but also those who do not exercise any discipline in the matter whatsoever. Not only the vacuous preachers instanced above, but there is also a general sloppiness of unawareness which is expressed by the use of such phrases as 'a short space of time', 'at this point in time'. These are of the same genre of that mental inactivity which can only express sympathy with those who have experienced some tragedy or other by having recourse to the tiresomely repetitive 'our hearts go out to them'.

This is no doubt a criticism of generally bad standards of expression and carelessness in language, but such commonly accepted phraseology is not only just an indication of the gliding over and refusal to look at what it is more appropriate to say, but an acceptance of supposed facts without any understanding of the real facts. What *does* 'at this point in time' mean? The very point, if there be such a measurement, has gone before the word has been completed and has no durance.

It may be said that I am being over-fastidious in this; yet it is a fact that common usage indicates a more serious general attitude of mind. In this case, space and time are regarded as mere conveniences and the import of existence in space and time – the real content of such sayings – glossed over and put aside for easier considerations.

Existence, and what space and time mean in that context, is also a general theme running through the discussion of all that follows. The theologian is concerned with the Existence of God and the existence which God has bestowed on his creatures. Above all – again as the main interpretative theme in this work – the existence of the Person of Christ, the Word made flesh, in whom we have to do with the Existence of God the Creator taking our created existence into unique union with himself as this Jesus Christ.

Here I would wish to approach another initial statement, developing that above that *place is significant space*. Theology should look at the question of space and time in terms of that Christological relation between our existence and the existence of God. This is its starting point. For here the created realities are seen in a unique way in the light of their Creator. The problem of space is then seen to be not a measurable one, but rather one of quality in terms of the nature of these existences, Divine and human, and the activity of the Person of the Word made flesh, the Creator taking our creatureliness to himself, the Infinite become finite, the Invisible, visible, the Incomprehensible, comprehensible, as Irenaeus constantly says.

In that Christological light, theology ought to see the issues of space and time concentrated, and from it make its particular contribution to the debate.

What, for example, does *came down from heaven ... ascended into heaven* mean in terms of the incarnation and ascension, for our concept of space? Does the Word journey in a measurable way to assume our creatureliness? Is it symbolic language? And if not, it surely cannot be construed as merely spatial, in the sense of measurable, terminology? The Nicene/Constantinopolitan Creed uses spatial terms in a distinctive way, as the whole hinterland of theological debate behind its formulation reveals. It is this usage and these concepts which are theology's contribution to the question of the nature of space and the temporal/spatial realities of which we are a part.

I would suggest, then, as the promised following initial statement to the assertion that *place is significant space*, that the significance of the place of the Person and activity of Jesus Christ is that in it we have a glimpse that *time is God's love and grace – expressed as His patience, the mindfulness He has – for us. Space is God's love and grace – expressed as His respect, the room He has – for us.*

There is a profundity and a wealth of insight in the Creed

which too long has been ignored as a source relevant to such matters as the nature of creation, and the significance of the spatial/temporal realities to that which gives them existence. Perhaps we should pause and think with sobering profit in the midst of all the speculation and discussion amongst the members of the relevant faculties and their graduated practitioners dealing with the mysteries of infinity and space and time and the nature of the universe, on Hilaire Belloc's observation[5]:

> ... *Credo in Unum Deum Patrem Omnipotentem, Factorem omnium visibilium atque invisibilium*; in which ... there is a power of synthesis that can jam all their analytical dust-heap into such a fine, tight and compact body as would make them stare to see.

Then we might appreciate and adopt the Psalmist's approach[6]:

> O Lord our Lord, how excellent is thy name in all the earth! who hast set thy glory above the heavens.
> When I consider thy heavens, the work of thy fingers, the moon and the stars, which thou hast ordained:
> What is man, that thou art mindful of him? and the son of man that thou visitest him?
> For thou hast made him a little lower than the angels, and hast crowned him with glory and honour.
> Thou hast made him to have dominion over the works of thy hands: thou hast put all things under his feet:
> O Lord, our Lord, how excellent is thy name in all the earth!

The infinite is not entered upon in immediate and heedless haste. The mystery of that which is above the heavens compels us to come down and look at ourselves and wonder that we should be so privileged as to have the awesome estate and vocation of humanity.

This was the approach advocated by Albert Einstein in looking at the incomprehensible immensities and complexities of creation[7]:

> that humble attitude of mind towards the grandeur of reason incarnate in existence, and which, in its profoundest depths is inaccessible to man ...

And before which[8]

all systematic thinking and acting as human beings is an utterly insignificant reflection.

This is not to say that we capitulate in face of the depths and complexities which confront us in exploring the nature of the universe and in asking questions about the nature of space and time, place and existence. But it does mean that we approach such with a mind that does not call its presuppositions truth and give its opinions the status of dogmas. Rather, the mind will let the inherent rationality of creation unfold itself in its integrity as we look at, and seek to understand, that universe in its various aspects, knowing that this is the proper function of humanity to which it is called.

So we enter the question of space. We note, for the first part, various ways in which that question has been approached, and then gradually enquire as to how theology may face the question and what it may contribute.

In the field of astrophysics, such questions are being addressed through all the data emerging from the Hubble telescope. I am given to understand that these centre round the value of the *Hubble Constant*. This is a rule of measurement, arrived at in the 1920s by the astronomer Edwin Hubble, for estimating the speed at which things are moving in the universe. There is no agreement at the moment as to whether the *Constant* should be seen as high or low – the higher the assessed figure, the quicker the universe is expanding, the lower the figure, the slower this process. This has important implications for an understanding of the beginning of the universe (and indeed the tenability of the Big Bang theory), its age and its nature, and in all the data forthcoming from the Hubble telescope, no doubt in a few years some of the answers will become less tentative. It is not for the theologian to trespass in other fields, but what is interesting in all this is the dynamic concept of the universe, and therefore the dynamism of space which is implied, and above all, the questions that are being put to widely accepted and facile ways of thinking about the nature of space and time, bringing them up short from their complacency. In what follows I am seeking to ask such questions from a theological standpoint.

1

The Theological Approach to Space

THE DEEPLY entrenched way of thinking in terms of idealized spatial and temporal concepts, stems in its more advanced form from Aristotelian and, to a certain extent, Platonic (or Platonic interpreted through Aristotelian preconceptions), philosophy. This essentially Greek mode of thought is one of the composite strands which, by their historical impact, have been formative of contemporary western modes of thought.

We owe much to the philosophy of ancient Greece, and that debt must not be dismissed sweepingly. But there are factors within that philosophy, particularly when it overcame its initial deep-rooted suspicion of a more mathematical as opposed to a metaphysical approach to the question of the infinite and its relation to the temporal/spatial dimension, which have had unfortunate consequences. The disjunction between form and content, the ideal and the natural reality, the spiritual and the corporeal, the theoretical and the natural, has produced an almost automatic dualism in our mental processes.

What we may call the heavenly, the divine, the eternal, is, on analysis, really the product of first a confusion, then a disjunction in our treatment of what we perceive as reality. It is but the projection to the *nth* degree of what we perceive as the formal truth of realities around us, but, because we are aware of the transient and corruptible nature of these, we remove from them their essential natural content and mentally construct ideal forms of them, shorn of all natural corruptibility. That means that we perceive the eternal or the divine in terms of idealized patterns and ultimately disparage the natural realities of our existence in their substance. Hence, in the popular mind, there is a separation of soul and body, heaven and earth, Creator and creature.

This particular way of understanding is a way of 'seeing'. It consists of formal perception, a looking at the form of things, an acceptance of things as they appear to us. The content of things is secondary to this primary understanding of them. Form and content are thereby divorced.

This lay behind much of the thought, both in philosophical application and in the common attitudes which that more academic emphasis inevitably formed as it permeated through and influenced all levels of mental application. It was a tendency which received renewed emphasis through the scholasticism of the middle ages, the approach centred on the so-called 'Cambridge Platonists' and the mechanistic idealism of Sir Isaac Newton of the 17th century, and the inaptly named 'Age of Reason' with its premise of the supposed autonomy of the mind of the 18th century. The legacy of Newtonian physics and rationalism still pervades and shapes many spheres of thought and activity in varied forms and diffusions.

How deeply entrenched it is may be instanced by the number of 'seeing' words used to denote understanding and truth. 'Evidence' (e video) in the Law Courts; the common phraseology 'do you see that?' for 'do you understand?' are but two of many examples from the whole spectrum of thought and expression from the precisely professional application to the unconscious common usage.

Equally deeply imbedded in our approach in thinking is that strand emanating from the civilisation of Rome. This is a pragmatic method of approach to realities. Their possible utilization and control by man dominates, directs and controls this mode of thought. Again, this particular legacy must not be disparaged. A considerable debt is owed to the administrative genius of ancient Rome which expresses itself in the historical legal, administrative and social structures of the West. The genius of the Latin mind was seen in its products – straight roads and an efficient communications and trading system, an appreciation of control and management of resources, clear and decisive laws underpinning the stature and quality of society at the height of conscientious Roman public life, a well-organized supply framework for far-flung armies and civil services, practical buildings, and so on.

This too, however, had and has its inbuilt dangers. Such practical endeavours which are meant for the benefit of the quality of life can become ends in themselves hedged about with self-justifications. They can assume an independent existence and a momentum of their own far removed from their original intent and purpose. The human ability to control, if it is separated from all due consideration of the nature of that which which it is dealing, can do violence contrary to the nature of that with which it is concerned.

The present day emphasis on *homo faber*, man the maker, the technological revolution, can acquire such a self-orientation out of context. It can foster an attitude which is concentrated on looking at things only in terms of their possible use, advantage and profit to the exclusion of all other concerns.

This is not to adopt a Luddite attitude and depreciate and dismiss all human achievement. But it is to point to a danger which lies in the bare combination of the two ways of thought from Greece and Rome, to the exclusion of other possible approaches. This manifests itself in an attitude of mind which idealizes by constructing formal theories and which, combined with the ability to manipulate and control with all mechanical and technical advance, expertise and fervour, may result in a malevolent technology which does violence to the natural quality and existence of things.

Nowhere is this perhaps so evident than in the sphere of humanity's attitude about existence – including human being, and perhaps particularly and most disastrously so – where utilitarian and expedient concerns can rise to the top. The Benthamite hollowness of the applied maxim of the *happiness of society* has caused more fundamentally pitiableness and anguish than can be recorded, for so much of that pain is unseen and, if it be recognized, then ignored for the sake of the ideal.

It is not without note that the 18th century, that period presumptuously, for all its resplendence, called the Age of Reason, with its emphatic rediscovery of classical expectations and priorities, still casts its influence insofar as its prevalent tenet concerning the autonomy of human reasoning is still determinative in so many areas of attitude and application.

It is this tenet of that autonomy of human reason which requires loosening and reforming. This is certainly so when we consider the nature of questions concerning space and time. Little commonly is done in thinking about and in exploring these apart from their measurement. Indeed the fundamental disparagement of them is that they are so commonly treated only as measurements of convenience. This question of the nature of space will be emphasized later.

At this point it is as well to recall that the thought forms of Greece and Rome are not the only strands in the present fabric of our way of thinking.

The third mode of historical thought which is part of the composition of our way of thinking is that which prevailed in certain areas and periods of intellectual achievement and resultant attitudes.

This is perhaps best exemplified historically in the disposition of the minds of the Nicene Fathers of the church in the 4th century (and particularly Irenaeus in the 2nd century before them) and may be typified as $\kappa\alpha\tau\grave{\alpha}$ $\phi\acute{\upsilon}\sigma\iota\nu$ – *kata phusin*, according to nature – thinking. That is to say the emphasis in this attitude of mind was that any thing had to be approached objectively, in accordance with its nature.

The truth about any thing, that is, what it is in itself, was to be allowed to reveal itself on its own terms. It was not to be approached by way of presupposition as to its possible nature, nor yet made to fit precipitately into any general scheme or theory.

On the contrary, the mind was to allow itself to be informed under the compulsive realities of the object as it revealed itself in all the authority of its own integrity. The truth about an object was to be expressed precisely in terms of the self-integrity of that object. It was not to be construed as any theory which could be imposed upon it on the basis of any authority other than the authority of that self-integrity.

In other words, in this way of thinking the mind was seen to be the hand-maid of truth rather than the master of it. The truth holds and is accorded the advantage here and is given priority over the examining and interpreting mind. The mind must reform and adjust itself in such a way that there is propriety of thought in accordance with the integrity of the object before it.

This Patristic way of thinking had a long hinterland of

pedigree. It was not confined to the fourth century. But in the fourth century the necessity was sharp for the church to be faithful in its interpretation out of Scripture as the witness to the fact, event and Person of the incarnate Word, Jesus Christ, in the face of Arian assertions concerning the nature of God's Self-Revelation, the Word made flesh.

Long before, Irenaeus saw with clarity the same necessity of propriety of thought and expression as he tackled the mythological systems of the various factions within Gnosticism. Hence he emphasises at the beginning of his *Demonstration of the Apostolic Preaching* the nature of truth and expresses this thus:

> Faith rests on things that truly are. For in things that are, as they are, we believe; and believing in things that are, as they ever are, we keep firm our confidence in them[1].

This κατὰ φύσιν way of thinking represents a cantus firmus, a constant fundamental, throughout that line of theologians culminating in Athanasius and Cyril of Alexandria in the fourth century, and from there remained an influence in subsequent thought which surfaced with profound results from time to time. The achievements of John Calvin, Francis Bacon and the Laudian Divines in the 16th and 17th centuries may be noted with the subsequent rise in the growth of natural science. Indeed, it was Francis Bacon who transferred Calvin's method of interpreting 'the books of God' to the scrutiny of the 'books of nature'. In the same way, the rise in natural science in the schools of fourth century Alexandria was hand in hand with the development of this objective mode of thought and practice emphasised by the theologians.

But even behind the Patristic emphasis on objective thought throughout the long line of theologians, lies that from which it took its character. This may be called the Biblical, or Hebraic way of thinking, and it is this which comprises the third strand which goes to contribute to our present attitudes of mind.

The whole epic of Israel is the unfolding of a people and of individuals confronted with the Self-revelation of God. Their resultant attitude was a matter not of thinking by 'seeing' or by way of manipulation and control, but of 'listening' and 'obedience'. *Hear, O Israel*. This is the confrontation of the mind and the totality of human being by the objective realities of God revealing himself in the experiences and circumstances of that people as the Creator who is 'beyond' the dimensions of space and time, yet nevertheless bears a relation to these dimensions as the result of the work of his hands. He is beyond comparison with anything within and of these dimensions:

> Who in the heaven can be compared unto the Lord? [2]

asks the Psalmist. Isaiah takes up the same question[3]:

> To whom then will ye liken God? or what likeness will ye compare unto him?

and reports God as asking[4]:

> To whom will ye liken me, and make me equal, and compare me, that we may be like?

Irenaeus, in his combat with Gnosticism with its confusion of temporal and spatial terms and values with the attributes of the divine, and applying to the Godhead that which properly belongs only to the created order in its limitations, emphasises this biblical insight of the incomparability of God with anything else, for all else is created[5].

> By their manner of speaking they ascribe those things which apply to men to the Father of all, whom they also declare to be unknown to all; and they deny that He Himself made the world, to guard against attributing want of power to him (that is, to safeguard any supposed weakness in the Creator for the fact that evil is within creation); while at the same time they endow Him with human affections and passions. But if they had known the scriptures, and been taught by the truth, they would have known, beyond doubt, that God is not as men are; and that His thoughts are not like the thoughts of men ... He is a simple, uncompounded Being, without diverse members, and altogether alike and equal to Himself, since He is wholly understanding, and wholly spirit, and wholly thought, and wholly intelligence, and wholly reason, and wholly learning, and wholly seeing, and wholly light, and the whole source of all that is good ... He is, however, above [all] these properties and therefore indescribable. For He may well

and properly be called an Understanding which comprehends all things, but He is not [on that account] like the understanding of men ... in all particulars the Father of all is in no degree similar to human weakness. He is spoken of in these terms according to the love [we bear Him]; but in point of greatness, our thoughts regarding Him transcend these expressions.

Athanasius, in his struggle against the Arian projection of the creaturely content of terms used about God into the Godhead and against the Son of the Father being regarded as the first of all creatures, supreme amongst them but nevertheless of the same dimension and therefore comparable with them, also took up this refrain of the impossibility of comparing God to any thing or anything to God[6]: He is

Beyond comparison.

This brings into focus the question of theological language – how we speak of this incomparable God. Here the Biblical way of thinking asserts itself. We can speak of God only on his own terms. *Only God speaks well of God* is a patristic dictum of fundamental importance and compelling direction. That is why the Self-Revelation of God, the Incarnation of the Word, where God confronts us in all his Goodness, without dilution, compromise, change or dismissal of his divinity, yet confronts us as this as the man Jesus, flesh of our flesh, blood of our blood and bone of our bone, in all the limitations of humanity within the temporal/spatial realities created by him as the eternal Word or Son, is the central and determinative doctrine of all doctrine. *What God is in himself, he is towards us in Jesus Christ* is the patristic follow-up to the first dictum.

Here in terms of the Word made flesh is theological language possible. But it is only valid theological language if it is in propriety to the nature of what it studies, namely that fact, event and Person of the Word made flesh. For it is here that God accommodates himself to our limitations and opens these limitations out, not to embrace and circumscribe within their bounds, but as pointers to, his divine and transcendent existence. That humanity may speak of God in terms of Jesus Christ who is THE Image of God, for he is what he images, is part of the ascription of humanity as being in the image of God.

It is propriety of thought and language with which we are concerned, as is clear, for example, in the quotation from Irenaeus above. But Athanasius too is exercised greatly by the need for terms suitable in theological usage – terms which, on the one hand, will not presumptuously seek to explain God away, encompassing him within the only language we have which, of necessity, is as limited as the spatial/temporal dimension of which we are a part and in which we live, move and have our being, while, on the other hand, it will be terminology called forth by the compulsion of the nature of the verity which confronts us, appropriate to that nature in as far as it can be.

The nature of theological language, therefore is that it is *paradeigmatic*, that is, that it points beyond itself, well aware of its limitations, to the objective verities of which it is speaking.

Perhaps this is best illustrated by instancing those former road signs, a wooden board shaped like a finger at the end. If we stood by one these and it signified by its pointing direction that Oxford lay that way, then we would know that we were not at Oxford, but sure that we were following the right direction to it.

How then is theology to begin to look at the concept and theological significance of the subject in hand – space? As with all aspects of the created dimension, theology can view it only in its relation to the Creator, and here we are concerned with the relation of the finite to the Infinite. But what can these terms mean theologically?

As far as theology is concerned, with regard to space, we can begin only at the space which God has made for Himself within our created dimension, the place and time of the Word made flesh. In this there are laid out the implications of the Infinite becoming finite without losing his infinity, or, as Irenaeus expresses it in speaking of the Incarnation[7]:

> Thus He took up man into Himself, the invisible becoming visible, the incomprehensible being made comprehensible

With regard to space and time, that line of theology which

ultimately expressed itself fully in the Niceno-Constan-tinopolitan Creed (in its first version after the Council of Nicea in A.D. 325 and its final version after the Council of Constantinople in A.D. 381) did not begin with the historical and prevalent philosophical notions of finitude and infinity. However, it used some of these, particularly Platonic and Neo-Platonic insights, to sharpen what it had clarified and evolved in a disciplined way of thinking from its biblical premises to which it constantly referred back its thought forms.

No doubt various fathers of the Church of the first four centuries dallianced with prevailing philosophical trends more closely than others – Origen with that of Aristotle is but one example. But that line which culminates in its fullest expression in the Councils of Nicaea and Constantinople is characterised by that biblical way of thinking which was its controlling norm, utilising the accomplishments of philo-sophical endeavour as its handmaid rather than its mistress.

Its thinking on space and time stems therefore from the Hebrew conception of *creatio ex nihilo*. But the insistence of this did not arise in its full perception merely from the Genesis narrative of creation. There, of course, such a doctrine is implied strongly, particularly through the use of the Hebrew verb *bara* to indicate God's creative action, as opposed to the use of *asah* employed indiscriminately to man and God's making something. *Bara* was reserved for God's act in bringing something into being which was not before.

The recognition of the importance of this distinction found expression in the theology of the Nicene Fathers. St Basil in his *Hexaemeron*[8] comments

> ... Moses does not use another word. 'In the beginning', he says 'God created'. He does not say 'God worked', 'God formed', but 'God created'.

Athanasius, too, countering the Arian claim that the Word was a creature, points out[9] that creatures make objects out of already existing substances. But the Word is not a creature; if he were, how

> is he able to frame things that are nothing into being? ... If then God also wrought and compounded out of materials,

> this indeed is a gentile thought, according to which God is an artificer and not a Maker ... But if He calls into existence things which existed not, by His proper Word, then the Word is not in the number of things non-existing and called.

Athanasius links three factors here. The first is that the Word, or Son, is co-existent with the Father, consubstantial, co-eternal. He is totally and utterly God. The second is that the Father made all things by Him; that is, there is an absolute difference between creation and the Word who is uncreated. The third is that these created entities have a beginning; the Word by whom they were made is eternal. The decree of God, *Let there be ... Let us make*[10], the act of God in creating, and the Person of the Word of God by whom all things are made, are profoundly bracketed together. God acts as He is; the Being of God is involved in the act. Creation is a dynamic and Personal event. The Word is uttered by the Father, the decree accomplished through that Word of the Father. This decree and this act result in an entity other than God – not eternal, but temporal, not infinite but spatial, not divine but created, not pre-existent but with a beginning.

Although this is partly explicit, partly implicit, in the Genesis narrative of creation, these fathers did not treat that as their sole or even primary source. Their interpretation of the act of creation is founded upon the Self-revelation of God in Jesus Christ, the Word made flesh, for there, in the place where God confronts humanity in the flesh without ceasing to be God, but accommodating Himself to human limitations and understanding, they perceived an entrance into the full implications of the creation narrative. Here was the Creator in the midst of his own handiwork, taking its realities into union with himself.

This is perhaps best set out in Athanasius's *De Incarnatione Verbi Dei*, for in this work, the Word as the one by whom all things were created is emphasised as the self-same Word who became incarnate, opening humanity out to the things of God and the knowledge of God and his works. The Creator of all who brought all things into existence out of nothing and who sustains all things by his mighty power accommodates himself to our limitations that we may be raised to that knowledge of the beginning and end of all creation, denied to us by these very limitations.

It is this 'place' of Jesus Christ, the Word made flesh, which is 'place' of all creation and all time and space – for they are recapitulate in him[11] – and which therefore is our vantage point and directive in thinking and speaking of space and time.

The substance and significance of all things, and thereby time and space, are grounded, not in themselves, but beyond themselves in the Creator Word of God. This is the essential and necessary fundamental theological declaration in the matter. Theology has looked at time and space not in terms of trying to perceive their significance out of themselves, but in the dynamic and Personal act of God, to whose Being the existence of all things bears a doubly contingent relation.

It is the doctrine of God so creating all things *ex nihilo* by his Word and sustaining them and fulfilling them by that self-same Word, which is the theological principle guiding and controlling all theology's thoughts about the nature of space and time.

The difficulties which arise in thinking about the nature of space and time spring from our failure to consider the doctrine of creation out of nothing as the head and pattern of such an exercise. Behind this lie several factors, mostly generated by the legacy of Greek and Roman thinking which forms such a part of our attitude to the objective realities of creation. This results in a failure to tackle the concept of *nothingness* except in terms of philosophical principles of a supposed infinity, gleaned from a mathematical/philosophical approach, or an entirely mundane dismissal of it as having nothing to do with practicalities.

The concept of *nothingness* has to be met and faced by theological discipline. We can begin only with the assertion that *In the beginning* there exists only God. There is nothing else. And because there is nothing else, there is no external compulsion upon God to create. Further, we simultaneously begin with the Self-revelation of God that He exists as Father and Son bound in the bond of divine love, the Holy Spirit. That is the *order*, the οἰκονομία, which the one God is in

Himself. He is in Himself all company, relation and love,
And because of this sufficiency, there is no internal compulsion on God to create.

Creation is thereby an act of God's grace creating an entity
other than himself but, in its created dimension in correspondence to the order of his divine Being, with its own
order and dimension. That order and dimension is finite, for
there is nothing infinite but God.

Just as it is nonsensical to speak of God creating 'in time',
so it is equally ludicrous to suppose that God creates 'in
space'. Time and space are not the eternal, pre-existent
medium in which the Word of God achieves the work of
creation. They are products of that act of creation. Nothingness has to be taken seriously.

But such is the resistance to dealing with the concept of
nothingness that there lurks as the presupposition to much of
our thinking about space that subtle acceptance of the mind
(by which we deceive ourselves into believing that we are in
control of such an undertaking) that there always was, is and
will be space – and time.

There is a tendency to begin, albeit subconsciously, with
the undisciplined and taken for granted view that there is an
infinity of space and an eternity of time. The very use of the
words *infinity* and *eternity* soothe the need to assure ourselves that we are not overwhelmed by, but can master, the
problem of space and time. For, even if we cannot reach the
end of this vaunted infinity and eternity, we have at least used
words to describe the problem to the satisfaction of the limitations of our minds, or to the comfort of our perplexity that
it really is only a question of mathematics which has a potential solution.

Either way, we are in fact saying that the question is one
on a plane not other than the mind's survey.

It is not. Once the doctrine of creation out of nothing is
taken seriously as the determinative of our thoughts about
space and time, then a much more radical problem confronts
us. We are brought up short by that *nothing* which is not just
empty space however vast or unfulfilled time however long,
but is negation of such qualitative difference – if words may
be used about it all – from any 'nothingness' which the mind

is capable of imagining even tentatively. It is the void of the void; the negation of every 'nothing'.

How do we approach this and how can we speak about it? Indeed, if it is such a negation, can we draw near to it at all and can we employ any terminology whatever if it is so beyond our thinking?

The answer is that we can neither approximate to it or find propriety of words to describe it – for it is not even 'it', but the negation of all.

We can only begin with God.

But the history of thought has thrown up a veritable regiment of theories about space. Theology should be aware of these, if for no other reason than that it should beware of some of them and see, given its basic premise and controlling mode of thought, where others can assist and clarify it in its task of looking at the concept of space as the medium where we live and move and exist. It is important that it does so, as it should do so with the concept of time. For this is part of its task to look, not only at the verities of the God who reveals himself in the incarnation of the Word, which is the substance of its proclamation and its raison d'être but also in the light of that revelation of God to gather up the rationality of creation as his handiwork and formulate a doctrine of creation which is commensurate with that dignity. In so doing it cannot avoid speaking also of the dignity of humanity in its role in creation and under God. Indeed it must do this. For in speaking about the self-revelation of God in the incarnation of the Word, it will have found that it must speak also of the fact that God has taken our humanity to Himself in that Word and declared it to be the object and sum of His creative and redeeming purpose for all that is.

Before embarking on a theological study of space, therefore, we look at various ideas of infinity and finitude in that history of human mental endeavour.

2

Some Historical Steps in the Concept of Space

IT SHOULD be a matter of note and pondering from the outset, that the terms employed in considerations of the infinite, and which thereby cluster round the unfolding of such endeavours, are generally in the first instance in the negative. In what may be called a *mathematical/philosophical* approach to the question of the infinite, such terms clearly are negations – *boundless, unlimited, immeasurable* and such like. Other terms are pressed into service in another attempted entrance to the question – *absolute, perfection, completeness* and similar – an approach which may be labelled the *ontological/philosophical*. This latter category of verbal concepts appears positive. But is it? I am indebted to A. W. Moore's *The Infinite* (Routledge, 1990) for some of what follows, with regard to directions in early philosophy.

The *mathematical/philosophical* attempt is concerned (as the nature of the choice of terms suggests) with measurement and infinity. The *ontological/philosophical* (again as that particular terminology indicates) seeks to deal with quality of existence and infinity. Clearly this distinction is one of emphases, for there are considerable areas of overlapping and mutual concern. Nevertheless, there is a radical difference in fundamental perception of approach to the question of the infinite. The first implies incompleteness with regard to infinity; the second fulfilment. Again, this would seem to indicate that the first is negative, the second positive. But is this so?

The first approach directs its negative content to the infinite, which is described in terms of 'un-something' or 'something-less'. But inasfar as the infinite is a goal sought, in a sense the world of temporal and spatial realities is forsaken and an implied criticism made of the fact that this created dimension is *bounded, limited, measurable*, and in this implied censure there is also a negative. So here is a double negation: infinity is that which finitude is not; finitude is insufficient for its very nature is a limitation to be overcome, even if only conceptually.

The second approach most certainly has a negative content by clear implication directed to the finite. For by direct contrast with what the infinite is conceived to be, the temporal/spatial realities are 'incomplete', 'imperfect', 'partial'.

It seems to me that both the mathematical/philosophical and the ontological/philosophical approaches are two sides of the one coin – and a counterfeit coin at that – for both rest, the one explicitly, the other implicitly, on what must, in the last resort, be a disparagement of the created realities, a reaction to what is observable, known and quantifiable. Perhaps the pointed observation of that fourth century father of the church, Gregory of Nazianzen, has some caution to offer from a parallel theological situation in his observation[1] with regard to the *via negativa* approach to God – the claim that we can describe God in terms of what the created realities are not – that if we cannot say positively what God is then we cannot say with any accuracy what he is not.

I pose this not out of any *odium philosophiae* or of devaluing philosophy's journeyings towards the infinite, but as a caution to philosophy from the discipline of theology. For, in like 'cause' of the infinite, theology has not been immune from a similar attitude of what can only be seen as dismissive of the integrity of the temporal and spatial realities, of what they are in themselves, of their self-integrity. This has been exhibited sometimes in the use of earthly symbolism drawn from nature to penetrate to the 'eternal verities'. Where there is a proper use of symbolism drawn from this source, the method of regarding created entities as merely transparent means to a greater end, disparages and discounts that significance and integrity. It abstracts a supposed significance from material things and this has damaging consequences for a demonstrative knowledge of what these things really are in themselves. The importance is laid on the thing only as a symbol of a greater verity, and reality becomes merely symbolic.

Robert Grosseteste in the 13th century saw the danger of

this usage of symbolism in theology clearly, and we will return to this later.

Suffice it to say here that theology (admittedly under an attitude of mind engendered principally by the emphasis on illumination and intuition through its uncritical absorption of Neo-Platonic thought) has, in various periods of history, stifled the cause of natural science.

But more; for in its more puritanical forms and periods, theology has been so obsessed with the 'infinity' and 'perfections' of God, that it has cast a very gloomy glance at what it should have been extolling as the handiwork of God, and has construed its purpose as setting forth the compensating harmonies of a perfect world 'above' as opposed to what it saw as the imperfect world 'below' – a sordid temporality. 'Original sin' was the watchword of such an attitude.

> All is a feeble shadow,
> A dream that will not stay;
> Death cometh in a moment
> And taketh all away.[2]

> A few more suns shall set
> O'er these dark hills of time,
> And we shall be where suns are not,
> A far serener clime.[3]

– are but two of the less vivid examples of such sentiments.

This cautionary counsel is offered, for there may lurk, secretive and unrecognized, an 'original sin' syndrome in some aspects of philosophic endeavours in the matter of the realm of the infinite. Perhaps, in Augustinian terms, a hereditary factory of early Greek thought as summed up by Anaximander of Melitus (c610–c546BC) towards spatial and temporal realities has passed through the generations of philosophers as a dark shadow! That particular father of thought about the infinite in Greek philosophy, in searching for the underlying fundamentum of all things, claimed that the primordial substance was the infinite which he conceived as the divine limitless source of all.

Change and decay in all around he saw, and, as his interest, in true puritanical vein, carried with it a determinative ethical concern, his interpretation of the spatial/temporal realities was one of repugnance. He saw the nature of these realities as an identity of discord, restless competition and variance, a continual vying one with the other for supremacy, of light being constantly consumed by darkness and darkness dispelled by light, of all the opposites in nature engaged in perpetual strife.

In all this restless activity and discord, Anaximander saw universal need and unfairness. Amends had to be made for all this. This retribution was accomplished through the judgment, punishment and atonement experienced by the spatial realities as in time they passed into the infinite from which they had sprung. The infinite was that in which there was perfect harmony and rest, for as these entities passed into the infinite, they lost in the process their competitively strifeful natures and identities which made them so deplorable in their relation one to another in Anaximander's pessimistic view.

There is an echo of this self-same attitude in the prayer of the 17th century Dean of St Paul's, John Donne:

> Bring us, O Lord God, at our last awakening into the house and gate of heaven, to enter into that gate and dwell in that house, where there shall be no darkness nor dazzling, but one equal light; no noise nor silence, but one equal music; no fears nor hopes, but one equal possession; no ends nor beginnings, but one equal eternity; in the habitations of thy glory and dominion world without end.

The view that created, material realities, at the worst, were essentially evil, or, at the best, of little consequence in themselves, did not hold universally in early Greek thought, though it did largely. Pythagoras (c.570BC ff) and his entourage took an opposing stand. He and they deemed the temporal/spatial realities to be essentially good, harmonious and ordered – at least some of them. Those which fitted their preconceptions of what such virtues were, were the opposite of the idea of the infinite. For they saw the infinite as a threat – as meaningless, without form and end or destiny.

Such temporal/spatial entities as well within the Pythagoreans' positive category they saw as overcoming and overpowering the surrounding infinite, a process in which order is construed as being brought out of meaninglessness, shape being formed out of formlessness. Here what was and is the normal form of dualism is reversed; the imperfect and bad was the infinite, the rational and the good the material world. However, not all of that world was regarded in such benevolent terms. Some entities within it fell under that meaninglessness category which had the infinite as its head.

There was a dualism within the created dimension – the ordered opposed to the imperfect, the singular opposed to the plural, the straightly linear opposed to the meandering curve, the odd numbers opposed to the even numbers, and even (among many other opposites) the male opposed to the female. Clearly – and it would not require deep or even hesitant feminist susceptibilities to judge this – the preconceptions of the Pythagoreans were arbitrary in the formulation of what was rational and what was not.

The point is that even here the integrity of the temporal/spatial realities was not appreciated on the objective grounds of what they were in themselves, but categorized according to other motives and considerations.

The disparagement of the created dimension was taken a stage further by Parmenides of Elea (c.515BC ff.) Although by training a Pythagorean, he became disenchanted with the view that the material dimension, the temporal/spatial order and structure, was held within a void which was construed as the infinite. He deduced that this meant that the reason for this dimension of time and things could only be ultimately stated in terms of what is not – the void of the infinite. He referred to reality as the *One*, and in so doing, drew a distinction sharply between reality and appearance.

His argument was that Reality did not change, for change means that things move from what *is* to what *is not*. No rationality can rest on what is not. Therefore Reality appears to us as an illusion, things changing, decaying, being dissolved in corruption. He did not hold that Reality was infinite, for what *is* must be complete.

The emphasis in Parmenides' direction of thought is on the ontological/philosophical, for in all talk of *completion*, mathematical infinity is ruled out, though it must be noted that neither did he hold a metaphysical or ontological concept of the infinite. He did not speak of Reality as the infinite, but offered a metaphysical or ontological analysis of Reality without direct appeal to the infinite. But his approach in distinguishing between appearance and reality is a disparagement and ultimately a dismissal of the created entities as they are in themselves.

However, the identification of reality in terms of an onto-logical or metaphysical infinite was but a step away. This was taken by Melissus of Sardis (fl. 5th century BC), a member of the Eleatic school, who declared the *One*, the reality of things as seen by Parmenides, to be the infinite. In so doing he drew out what was latent in Parmenides' thought, the logical line of which demanded this conclusion. For to describe reality, the One of all things as apart from their transitory and corruptible appearance, as *changeless* means that that One is *timeless* (as Parmenides suggested without developing this). This 'eternal' attribute can only mean the metaphysically infinite reality (as this word is construed by Parmenides and Melissus) of all things.

This open assertion by Melissus that the 'eternal' and 'indivisible' One – what all things really are despite their appearance – is infinite, heightened that disparagement of the created entities. This is an ontological/philosophical approach to the concept of the infinite; it is not mathemati-cal, for the One was regarded as not extendible, being indi-visible, and a unity not composed of parts, which separation into parts was but the appearance of things. Melissus widened even further the distinction and division between 'reality', now elevated into the infinite, and the appearance of this temporal/spatial dimension.

Change, and therefore motion, was regarded as unintelli-gible by Parmenides and his followers. Another member of the Eleatic school, Zeno (c.490BC) took this up in his four supposed 'paradoxes'. The point of these 'paradoxes' is not to set out two opposing but equally valid arguments, but to demonstrate the absurdity of mathematical infinity and the approach to such a concept. This he does by setting an analy-sis of motion and its measurement over against that which does happen. For example (to reduce his argument, simplis-tically perhaps, but to pinpoint the essence of it), the distance between A and B can be regarded mathematically as composed of a half, a half of a half, a half of that, ad infinitum. But this is absurd because we could never, in leaving A, arrive at B. We do. Reality cannot be approached in this way.

In Parmenides, Melissus and Zeno, we find the rejection of the mathematical infinite. Reality is not boundless, immeasurable, unlimited. It may be, in Parmenidean terms, 'eternal', but it is even here construed as being thereby present in its totality at any one time.

I have said above that the mathematical/philosophical approach bears with it a basic disparagement of the temporal/spatial realities. The inclination of these philosophers would seem to bear this out. But equally, the ontological/ philosophical approach can have the same effect. The radical disjunction between 'reality' and 'appearance' (and therefore 'experience') comes about when the meaning of these entities is sought in an artificial framework of indivisibility, eternity and infinity, imposed upon them without little or any reference to objective thought as to the integrity of what they are in themselves and in their relation one to the others. Even the Pythagorean approach of seeing such entities as good, depends on a highly selective attitude towards them, placing them within a like arbitrary framework of selection which has no regard for their intrinsic natures.

At this point I would wish to point to the κατὰ φύσιν way of thinking outlined above – that is, that way of thinking wherein the objective verities of this dimension in which we live, move and have our being and of which we are a part, are allowed to reveal their intrinsic natures – as a corrective.

I do so, not by way of criticizing the philosophers already mentioned, for this objective way of thinking was a long way ahead of them in the history of the development of thought. What I do wish to question and see as needing a corrective, is the tendency to seek reality in what is ultimately a denial of the limitations of these entities and of our own finitude, by elevating in the last resort what they are not as though that is what they really are. The caution of Gregory Nazianzen, that we cannot know what something is not without first accurately saying what it is, is apposite here. To speak of the nature of the temporal/spatial realities in terms of what they objectively are in themselves and on that basis to seek reality

and the whole context of their existence, is that way of thinking according to nature.

Something of humility of mind is required, not only in
letting the mind be informed by the external verities, but also
in pondering the fact that the truth of an object resided in
that object before I began speaking about it, resides there
when I am speaking about it, and will remain there long after
I have spoken about it. But above all, that truth of that object
will remain exactly what it is in its integrity whatever I say
about it.

This recognition also implies a further recognition of the
limitations of the mind. This, too, is something which theology has sometimes forgotten. Lancelot Andrewes (1555–
1626), Bishop of Winchester, complained[4] of those in his day
who presumed that they knew the mind of God and had
measure of it:

> ... this sounding the depths of His Judgements with our line
> and lead; too much presumed upon by some, in these days of
> ours ... (Saith the Psalmist) His Judgements are the great
> deepe. St Paul, looking downe into it, ranne backe, and cried,
> O the depth! the profound depth! not to be searched, past our
> fadoming or finding out. Yet there are in the world that make
> but a shallow of this great deepe: they have sounded it to the
> bottome. God's Decrees, they have them at their finger ends,
> can tell the number and order of them just, with 1, 2, 3, 4, 5.
> Men that (sure) must have beene in God's Cabbinet, above
> the third heaven, where St Paul never came.

The recognition of the finitude of the mind is an emphasis
which has emerged from time to time in the history of
thought. Even if one does not agree with the total direction
and aim of some of the philosophical systems with which this
is associated, it is heartening to see it, even if it be only a salu-
tary reminder and rebuff to those who would stretch exces-
sively beyond their station in life, which is the mortality of us
all! Sometimes those who noted the limited capacity of the
mind paid little heed to their self-confessed strictures as they
soared aloft in an ecstacy of compensation, turning their
limitations into that which reeks of the absolute – as the
rather sad spectacle of the arrogance of some existentialists
bears witness.

Be that as it may; our concern here is with the limitation of the mind vis-a-vis the idea of infinity. So Thomas Hobbes (1588–1679), who was direct in his criticism of – bordering on cynicism towards – those who bandied the term 'infinity' about, and who applied it as a description of some *thing*. They were, he averred, merely indulging in a commentary on their own limitations and total incapacity to perceive an end to that thing which they were so describing. In other words all talk about infinity highlighted human finitude and mental limitation.

There is in Hobbes a considerable (though perhaps unconscious, springing as it did out of his materialistic emphases) move in support of objective thinking and the necessity of recognizing what things were in themselves. This, however, was subjectivised in terms of perception through experience. He believed that we could not think adequately of something which we had not already, even if only partially, experienced and grasped. Thus any attempt to deal with the infinite was ruled out of the realm of the possible.

Hobbes and Rene Descartes (1596–1650) did not agree on certain fundamental approaches concerning the infinite. The latter, though he believed that God was solely the true, actual Infinite, and that He had placed within us an idea of the infinite, could warn that because of the finitude and mortal capacity of the mind, our thoughts could only impinge on the infinite. We could never circumscribe it with our mental ability, but we could by reason contact the infinite even if it was beyond our mortal ken and experience.

Unfortunately what stemmed from Descartes' dictum *cogito ergo sum* as a core of absolute certainty, rather detracts from the apparent recognition of the limitations of the mind.

This direction towards κατὰ φύσιν thinking is found in Blaise Pascal (1623–1662) in an more emphatic, yet humble and thereby more telling, way.

It deserves to be resurrected from its comparative obscurity outside philosophical circles into a revitalisation of its full significance. He dwelt on the reverence, awe and respect one ought to have of nature in its immensities and intensities, that is, in its macroscopic and microscopic realities. We are utterly incapable of subsuming these within the bounds of our minds. They are beyond imagining and fathoming out in their full significance. The temporal and spatial realities he regarded as

> an infinite sphere whose centre is everywhere and circumference nowhere,

but these infinite extremities meet and conjoin in God alone. The human mind may reach out to this sphere and think about it in a way which elevates and dignifies us beyond our limits – but without de-humanising and dissolving by over-reaching what we are in ourselves. Our finitude is endowed, through the rational processes, with the finding of its identity in that context of what to us is infinite, but what is, as infinite to us, contained and encompassed in the Being of God.

Now Pascal's observations may be seen as reaching both backwards and forwards and, unbeknown to him, moving in the same direction as two other significant lines of thought in the epic of grappling with the infinite. Backwards it stretches in its parallelism to the thought of Robert Grosseteste (c.1170–1253) with his insistence that all our infinities – for such they appear to the limitations of the mind – are but finite to God being utterly dependent upon Him.

> sicut enim que vere finita sunt, nobis sunt infinita, sic que vere in se sunt infinita, illi sunt finita[5].
>
> For just as those things which in fact are finite in themselves, and to us they are infinite, so things which in fact are infinite in themselves are finite to Him.

Forwards it reaches to Albert Einstein (1879–1955) with his emphasis that as we penetrate towards the mysteries of the universe in their macroscopic and microscopic realities, we cannot but appreciate a marvellous intelligibility which is far vaster than the comprehension of our finite minds. So Einstein speaks of

> That humble attitude of mind towards the grandeur of reason incarnate in existence, and which, in its profoundest depths is inaccessible to man[6].

The rapturous amazement at the harmony of natural law, which reveals an intelligence of such superiority that, compared with it, all systematic thinking and acting of human beings is an utterly insignificant reflection[7].

David Hume (1711–1776), likewise, noted that the capacity of the mind being limited

can never attain a full and adequate conception of infinity.

Hume's contribution, as far as the direction which I am pointing out here in the question of the limitations of the mind is concerned, is the relation between space, time, infinity and experience. His empiricism led him to the view that experience was of the same substance as the spatial/temporal realities, experience being composed of minute, indivisible 'parts' firmly anchored within this spatial/temporal dimension. The ontological/philosophical approach of Hume, and the disregarding and eventual discarding of any mathematical/philosophical attempt, led to a steadfast view of the finitude of things, humanity and the capacity of the human mind included.

But this – which was essentially an 'atomistic' approach to reality – left untouched the question of the *significance* of space and time and all things within the spatial/temporal dimension. For such empiricist approaches must, in the ultimate resort, be obliged to find the reason and unifying principle of meaning within the created realities themselves. One has to ask if this is not a task equally impossible as that of struggling with the infinite. Indeed, it may be further asked if this is not a case of extreme and unwarranted 'glorying in one's infirmities', and, in the throwing overboard of any idea of infinity, elevating the mind as the master of all it surveys to occupy the vacancy!

Be that as it may; the factor of the finitude of the mind cannot be ignored, and, on that basis a direction set in the attempt to grapple with the question of the infinite and the nature of space and time.

We turn to look at the concept 'infinity' as it has been employed by various Christian thinkers in relation to its Greek philosophical background.

3

The Concept 'Infinity'

RICHARD SORABJI's robustly able defence of late Neoplatonism[1] is aimed at countering the opinions of some that that philosophical school had become arid and dead, and that this was the justification for the emperor Justinian's closure of the Athens school of philosophy in AD529. In so aiming, he chooses to examine the work of John Philoponos, a Christian trained in the Neoplatonist School of Alexandria, and in particular concentrates on this thinker's attack on, and answer to, the Aristotelian concept of infinity.

Sorabji makes no apology for choosing a Christian to illustrate his thesis as to the liveliness and influence of late Neoplatonism. His point is that there was considerable overlap between Christian theology and Neoplatonic thought. Philoponos made use of the philosophical training and emphasis in which he had been nurtured in Alexandria, in order to further his theological observations.

He lauds Philoponos not for settling the question of infinity, but for turning the argument of the Aristotelians upon themselves, thus exposing the questionable ambiguity of their thought on the matter. He describes Aristotle's view of infinity as an *extendible finitude*[2], seeing the summing up of his attitude in his observation[3]:

> For in general infinity exists through one thing being taken after another, what is taken being always finite, but ever other and other.

This concept of infinity raises many problems. Are these things to be taken like points on a line which are marked off one after another? Sorabji sees an affinity between Aristotle's concept and more modern approaches to the question – the modern idea of *approaching a limit* being similar, where 1 is approached by marking off a half, a quarter (a half of the half), an eighth, and so on. The finite procedure goes on, but

1 is never reached, for yet more and more divisions of points can be added.

But if this is the case, then is there not here a further question? Is it a matter of marking off on a line points already in existence, or a matter of bringing them into existence? Aristotle, in Sorabji's view, believes that infinity is a matter of a succession of things coming into existence in actuality one after another[4]. However, the problem deepens; for we may then ask that while there may be actual divisions on a line perceived and made, what of potential divisions? Aristotle claims[5] that unlike the then received idea of infinity – which was that it was so pervading that nothing was outside it – it always has something outside it. Hence one can always take a progression of yet more and more.

Aristotle regards infinity in terms of actual divisions made on a line and added to ever and again. This is because he regards infinity as – as I see it and if I may use the word in a singular sense – pure. That is to say, he will not countenance many infinities, or a compound infinity made up of infinities. Sorabji believes that it is because of this that he did not admit potential divisions or points on a line other than finite points and therefore finite divisions which may be marked off, for this would mean that there is an infinite number of points within any division and the divisions would thereby also be infinite. Infinity would then be an absurd infinite collection of infinities.

The outcome of this is that for Aristotle, infinity itself is *potential*, while the constituent finite parts of which it is composed solely, are *actual*. The actualities by being increased constantly move towards infinity – hence infinity is an *extendible finitude*, to use again Sorabji's own succinct and clear phrase.[6]

Yet, as Sorabji points out, when Aristotle comes to deal with one of Zeno's 'paradoxes' of half divisions, he has to make *an important qualification* to his assertion that because infinity is potential and never actual[7] it can never be traversed[8]. This particular paradox deals with the question of one moving towards a goal. The example is that of Achilles, having given a tortoise a head start of a given measurement, races it and attempts to overtake it, but on reaching the point where the tortoise was cannot overtake it, for in the time he takes to do so, the tortoise has moved on already. The same fundamental problem is instanced by a person moving from a point in a room to go to a door. The half distance from the beginning point to the desired end of the movement will have to be traversed, then the half of that and the half of that. The goal will never be reached! Or, again, we could cut a loaf of bread in half, eat that, then cut half of the half left, consume that, return later to the half of the half and cut that in two equal parts, and so on. We would never finish the loaf! Yet, manifestly, Achilles does overtake the tortoise, we do arrive at the door and we do eat the whole loaf, and in so doing in these respective examples we have traversed an infinity of divisions. Zeno's 'paradoxes' are designed to illustrate his doctrine, taken from Parmenides, that reality is indivisible and that reason is at variance with the senses. The 'paradoxes' are designed to show absurdity.

Aristotle seeks to solve the problem raised by this 'paradox' by saying[9] that despite the fact that we cannot go through an infinity of divisions actually existing, we can go through an infinity of potentially existing ones. But this allows more than a finite number of potential divisions and manifestly contradicts what he has said about potential infinities being composed only of finite actual divisions in *Physica 3*. For in so allowing these he can only raise the spectre of divisions which are themselves infinite. It is this inconsistency surrounding the traversing of an infinity which Philoponos exploits. This Philoponos does by pointing out that the universe must have had a beginning. Those who agree with Aristotle that there is no actual infinity, must yield to the fact that the universe indeed has a beginning, otherwise they contradict themselves since, if it had no beginning it would already have gone through an actual infinity of years. Here Time and Space coalesce in consideration.

Two things may be said about this 'infinity'. First that if there were no beginning to creation, this infinity could not be a potential infinity in Aristotelian terms, for some starting point must be made for such to be the case. It is not enough to say that the present is the starting point and work back a potential infinity from there. In any case the present is not itself static, unmoveable. But more importantly, this leads to the second point, that if the universe had no beginning, not only would an infinity have already been passed through, but it would be an infinity of years plus one because of next year. Infinity plus is absurd.

Sorabji outlines Simplicius's answer to Philoponos – that there is not an actuality of an infinity of years, for the years pass away. They no longer exist. They only exist as finite divisions; they do not remain and therefore there is no question of an infinite collection – an actual infinity – of them. They are increased and are therefore a potential infinity, since an actual infinity, by virtue of the fact that past years do not exist, equally does not exist. Here, it should be noted, Simplicius's reply to Philoponos relies on the lame and dubious notion that past years do not exist merely because they are not present.

However, as Sorabji goes on to point out, Aristotle himself permitted the thought of potential divisions as entities in *Physica 3* and he is surely committed logically therefore to acknowledge that past years do form, if the world is without beginning, such an infinite collection, even if he had protested that it be a potential infinity.

By this argument it would seem that Philoponos has exploited successfully the inherent contradiction in Aristotelian thinking that if there is no beginning of time then this must mean an actual infinity of years which has been gone through already, and not, as Aristotle would have it, a potential infinity of years which can be increased because it is an extendible finitude.

It seems to me that Philoponos is emphasising the idea that a supposed infinity of years cannot be treated as an *extendible finitude*, for that must surely depend, since finitude is present, on a beginning, or on a static point from which we can refer back – a point which is a beginning in another sense, but no less fixed. To this I will return in noting where Sorabji himself brings it up in the development of his objections to Philoponos's rebuttal of Aristotelian thought that it is impossible for an infinity to be actual or gone through.

To return to Philoponos and his thesis against an 'increasable', 'beginningless' infinity: it must be underlined that if the world is without beginning, an actual infinity has been passed through, and this Aristotle denies. Of course his self-contradiction in *Physica 8* allowing an actual infinity of potential divisions, may well indicate that he himself was ill at ease with the matter of potential and actual infinities.

Sorabji himself suggests that Philoponos was wrong in claiming that infinity cannot be increased – that to have infinity plus is absurd. This he does in a most ingenious way. This consists of distinguishing that there is a sense in which infinity can be conceived as 'increasable' (my word, not Sorabji's) and a sense in which it cannot.

He addresses the question in terms of whether one infinite collection can be larger than another, and may be so regarded, by being increased. His illustration is that of an infinity of *whole* numbers against an infinity of *odd* numbers. He asks us to imagine two aligned columns – a column of whole numbers stretching out infinitely from the sight of the left eye, and a column of odd numbers likewise from the sight of the right, the numbers 1, 2, 3, 4 and so on in the left column matching the numbers 1, 3, 5, 7, etc.

Sorabji claims that the column of whole numbers will not be larger than the column of odd numbers, because since neither column has a far end, *it will not stick out beyond the far end*[10] of the column of odd numbers. But there is the other sense in which the column of whole numbers is larger than that of the odd numbers; it contains the odd numbers *and more besides.* He seizes upon the terms *beyond* – as in *not sticking out beyond the end of* – and *besides* as in *containing more besides.*

Following John Murdoch, the science historian, he finds that this distinction between *beyond* and *besides* has a hinterland of usage, traceable to the fourteenth century and the works of Henry of Harclay, William of Alnwick, William of Ockham and Gregory of Rimini (though he is careful to say that he may be over-simplifying these persons' use of the Latin terms *ultra* – *beyond* and *praeter* – *besides*).

With regard to the last two named, the terminist logic expounded by William of Ockham and taken up in development by Geoffrey of Rimini, whereby a distinction was drawn between two kinds of statements and two kinds of meaning, has to be considered in any statement about infinity, otherwise over-simplification of such minds can be indeed the danger.

This will be commented on below; but in the meantime we turn to Sorabji's development of his dealing with Philoponos's rebuttal of Aristotelian claims regarding actual infinities and their traversing.

In this development he lists several objections which have been raised, and might be called upon in support of Philoponos's claim that the universe had a beginning and therefore has not gone through an actual infinity of past years.

Although supporting Philoponos's arguments against Aristotelian thought by exposing the inherent contradiction in that particular approach to a beginningless creation, Sorabji does not necessarily stand with Philoponos in his arguments for the beginning of creation. He leaves the question as to a beginning or an infinite past open, in that he has no objection to the proposition that an actual infinity can be gone through – a proposition, Aristotle's contradictory approach having been dealt with, to which he has no objection.

The first objection is that if an infinity of days had to pass, or be traversed, before today arrived, there would never be a 'today'. He counters this by saying that if there is no first day, there is room enough for a preceding infinity to allow today its place.

The second is in regard to the matter of counting infinity, which, of course could only be an imaginary exercise by some imaginary beginningless being with a beginningless counter. The objection is that, given no beginning, such a count already would have come to infinity at any year chosen at random. So this infinite counting could never be finished.

He counters this by pointing out that counting must not be confused with *traversing*, that is going through the infinity of years, in that, in order to count, one must begin with a first number which corresponds to the first member in the series. But this cannot be so in a beginningless series. Indeed this 'normal' counting is impossible with regards to infinity, precisely because there is no starting year and therefore no corresponding number with which to begin the count.

Sorabji claims that this is no difficulty to the concept of traversing an infinity of past years, again precisely because there is no starting year in the series.

I presume that by this Sorabji means that the universe has gone through, traversed, the infinity of past years, which infinity is actual. I further presume that this distinction between counting and traversing is in the same sense that the Zenonian type paradox of reaching the door in theory means that we can never reach the door by counting half the distance and half that, ad infinitum, yet will in fact reach the door. The underlying distinction in all this, of course, is between the ontological and the mathematical.

He does suggest that there could be a singular method of counting, as opposed to the straightforward one, by which method God's imaginary beginningless meter recorded how many years there were until – the instance Sorabji gives – the Incarnation, at which point the meter would read zero. As he points out this would not be normal counting, for the count would never have been begun, but it is conceptually possible in principle. There is no logical barrier to this form of counting, and therefore no such barrier to traversing an actual infinity of years.

The third point emphasises that for those who claimed a beginningless universe, an infinity of years was always infinite. There was never a question of turning a finite series into a completed infinity by merely adding a further number. I presume again that he means that Aristotle's extendible finitude is not such an attempt to jump from the finite to the infinite by extending the number, but that this is the process within infinity already there.

In the fourth point, Sorabji instances Bonaventure's objection that anyone thinking back from the present over past years will never reach an *infinitieth* year. Again he points out that this is a mistaken view of what those who claim a beginningless universe set out regarding an infinity of years. A year did not occur an infinite number of years ago. Infinity relates to the whole, not to one within the series of years. If there were a year which was the infinitieth one, then the whole would not be infinite.

The fifth point seeks to dismiss the objection which had

been raised in Islamic thought, that by virtue of being infinity, the infinite cannot reach a terminus and therefore its completion. He answers this by observing that an infinite series can have one end, as the collection of even numbers does at zero. In the case of past years that end is the present.

His sixth observation is that there is a *disanalogy* between an infinity of past years and an infinity of future ones. Past years do not begin at the present; rather, it is our thoughts about them which so begin. Here Sorabji develops his argument about the acceptability of one terminus for an infinity of years. That there should be one end – and, it is to be noted, not two – means that they have been gone through as an infinity of past years which is more than an extendible finitude.

On the other hand, with regard to future years, these have a starting point – the present – and if we speak of a series of such years as having been gone through, we would be crediting them with a finishing point as well. So we would have two termini, and it is this which prevents those future years which are so traversed (and only those traversed) between the two points from being other than finite.

In other words, the past, because we give it an end, namely the present, has been traversed. Only of a finite number of future years from the present to whatever end we choose can it be said that they have been gone through at that chosen point. Only if future years had – impossibly – arrived at a point which was infinitely distant from the starting point of the present could they be an actual infinity. Herein lies the difference between the term infinity as applied respectively to past and future.

Sorabji's seventh point underlies the necessity of distinguishing between *infinitely many* and *all*. The first term does not include, or even imply, the latter. He reverts to the observation that an infinity of *odd* numbers is not an infinity of *all* numbers. An infinity of past years is quite a permissible argument in Sorabji's estimation, for it does not imply an infinity of all years, past years having an end though not a beginning.

In his final point, he also appeals again to the observation he made in respect of two infinite columns (that is, for example, a column of whole numbers and one of odd numbers) not being larger than the other because the one does not stick out farther than the other at the 'end'. This dismisses any claim that the idea of an actual infinity is an argument inevitably *ad absurdum*.

By these points, Sorabji seeks at least not to dismiss the concept of a beginningless universe, and that of an actual infinity, bearing in mind Philoponos's exposé of the Aristotelian method of claiming such a creation without beginning in terms of an infinity which is but an extendible finitude.

I now wish to look at the issues so raised from the theological point of view. To do so, I make an entrance into this by turning to the substance of some of the works of William of Ockham or Occam (c1285–1347). My reason for doing so is that these exhibit clearly, even though implicitly, a way of thinking about abstract concepts through a general approach to ways of knowing, which gave impetus to much misconception in the later mediaeval trend in dealing with the question of what knowledge is and how it is gained.

Ockham's theses further seem to me, from the entanglement which he and followers of them caused, to demonstrate the necessity of exposing the essential differences between the respective basic approaches of what is strictly systematic theology and that of philosophy in general towards knowledge and handling of concepts such as infinity – all this, of course, from what I hope is the courteous address of one discipline to another, from systematic theology with all respect for the Faculty of Philosophy and an acknowledgement of its immense contribution towards theological endeavour.

I begin this with the Occamist doctrine of the nature of knowledge. This speaks of a division between intuitive and abstractive knowledge. It states that intuitive knowledge leads to *direct statements* or *signification*, in which the meaning lies in reference to the objects of intuitive experience, in their pointing to these objects.

This intuitive knowledge is distinct from abstractive knowledge. The latter leads to statements of *supposition*, whereby terms and statements are detached from any objects of reference, and are regarded not as paradeigmatic, that is pointing to objects and thus signifying them, but as abstract and substitutionary for things signified. The emphasis here is on the function of words in their relation to one another (their *complexes*, as Ockham called it), and in terms themselves, without any paradeigmatic content or purpose, as linguistic tools for developing thought and as units of mental abstractions.

Parallel to this distinction, and complementary to it, is Ockham's division of *first intentions* and *second intentions*.

First intentions, or *intentia recta*, are the response of the mind to the confrontation by objective realities – things as they are in themselves – *ad res ad extra*. This category of first intentions is composed of objective fact and subjective perception – the external object and the perceiving soul. What is expressed under this category is the state of the soul in perception of the objective reality. That expression is the act of the soul signifying, pointing to, the external object, and as such it is a paradeigmatic expression.

Second intentions, or *intentia obliqua*, are concerned with expressions about expressions; they are concerned with the relations of ideas rather than the signification of things. They have neither objective reference nor concern for the state of the soul perceiving objectivities, for they are propositions which only have meaning in conjunction with other propositions in the mind's particular employ.

These two – first and second intentions – may be categorized as the relation of the soul (the thinking subject) to objective realities and to the relation of ideas, respectively.

However, this distinction between intuitive and abstract knowledge was not upheld as though between equal, and indeed even complementary, ways of knowing. For it is evident that William of Ockham veered towards the latter way of abstractive knowledge and the placing of logic solely and firmly within the realm of language, divorced from any necessity of verifying any proposition against empirical concerns. Certainly his devotees stressed also the importance and role of the second intentions, the *intentia obliqua* over against the *intention recta*, and this heightened the interest and emphasis on looking for truth in terms of the development of logic and the use of oblique terminology deflected from the nature of the realities under scrutiny.

Ockham himself, despite his laudable attempt to categorize both intuitive knowledge and first intentions and thus safeguard objectivity (compromised as this attempt was by his over-anxious desire to give the thinking subject, the comprehending soul, its place) emphasised that ultimately we can only know propositions, and of such is all science composed. Indeed, even in his first double category of intuitive knowledge paralleled with first intentions, the emphasis there is on the state of the thinking soul, rather than the objectivities perceived by that soul, for he claimed that we are more certain of the former than the latter.

In fairness to Ockham, he saw the difficulties raised by the whole scheme of the mediaeval synthesis of knowledge, but only worked within that scheme, seeking a solution from within, and was thus ultimately constrained by it. What was required was a radical questioning of the assumptions behind that scheme. Ockham thus eventually only intensified what he sought to loosen.

This view of Ockham and this split between intuitive and abstract knowledge in favour of the latter, had several and severe repercussions. Some of these, such as that concerned with the authority of the Church in relation to the knowledge of God, are not our concern here. But two of them are.

The first is the fact that terms themselves, once defined, become the objects of our knowledge. The role of theology was thereby perceived to be the definition and clarification of such abstractions as are woven into, and reside in, Scripture and Tradition – the *creditive ideas* as Ockham called them. Faith and reason were only tenuously linked by the formalism of logic and grammar.

The second, stemming from this, is the ultimate capitulation to the idea of the autonomy of the mind – even if that idea is covert and unstated. The mind becomes the court of authority and final appeal.

I now wish to set beside these observations on what I see as the repercussions in Occamist thought as an example of having to be aware of the philosopher's assumptions under the compulsion of formal logic, a theological critique of what might be called a *philosophical infinity*, and these assumptions of philosophy in approaching such a concept.

It seems to me that the danger for the philosopher and more particularly the formal logician, is that what he or she calls 'Infinity' can become an abstraction which in the last resort is a formulation of the unquestioned scope of the mind wrestling with propositions. These propositions, because they are abstractive, are self-propagating and self-perpetuating. Again we are faced with the ontological and mathematical distinction, the latter taking priority in the approach to the concept of Infinity. Moreover, because such are abstractions of the mind, the mind itself holds court and has the priority. It must be asked if the proposal and manipulation of these abstractions, as opposed to the mind confronted with objective realities and in propriety disciplining itself to the priority of what these realities are in themselves, is not, secretly, an assertion of its self-ascribed autonomy and an avoidance of the recognition of its limitations. Is this not the mental equivalent of the creation of an indispensible but artificial bureaucracy dedicated to self-perpetuation and making impregnable the position of the 'middle man' – the mind?

Is there not here – even if dormant – the assumption of the unassailable and unquestionable priority of the mind over against all knowledge?

This is not to say that all philosophy is an unwarranted exercise in unreality and artificiality. Far from it. Sorabji is an honest philosopher and will not admit via philosophical means to the proof of either a beginningless universe or one with a beginning. But the emphasis on the mathematical/philosophical approach is the trouble.

Yet this very admission is a laudable reminder of the limits and role of philosophy in its mathematical approach. But the danger is that not all are so honest and that unless in some areas of philosophy its concepts and language are seen in necessary relation to existence, as Heidegger has pointed out, then in the damage so done, language and concepts become obscure. Or, unless these concepts and terms are grounded in objective thought and constantly referred back to the reality of things as they exist in themselves, they can take on an artificial existence of their own and exercise an unwarranted but compelling attraction.

Intentia obliqua take precedence over *intentia recta*; formal logic over objective (or κατὰ φύσιν, according to nature) thinking, the mathematical over the ontological.

Philosophy's high aim of logically pursuing the bases of knowledge and ultimate reality and refining thought about what is suggested by objective integrities, and the relating of language to reality, can degenerate into something as useful as drawing pictures on water.

This charge may of course be countered by the question 'What is reality and therefore objectivity?' I would only here counter that in return by reminding the questioner of Dr Johnson's observation to the solipsist who believed that he alone existed and that all else was an illusion for his benefit – which advice was that he should take off his shoe and kick the nearest rock.

The term *infinity* could be seen to have become such an abstraction attracting endless debate! Indeed it could unleash a self-generating industry which would keep a countless regiment of philosophers unceasingly occupied. As a theological corrective to this we will turn later to Robert Grosseteste's observations on the concept. But, before doing so, I wish to pick up certain points made above.

We may ask, even of Sorabji's approach, if the role of the thinking individual has not been accorded its full propriety. By this I do not mean to imply that a supposed autonomy of the mind should be magnified. Rather, it is a question of the place/time significance of the individual in relation to the supposed infinity, whether potential or actual which he or she is contemplating.

If we live and move and have our being in an infinite time/space universe, are we in a position at all to grasp rationality? I would adhere firmly to that position taken by orthodox doctrine, typified by the fourth century Nicene Fathers of the church, that creation had a beginning and that it will have a fulfilment. If it has no beginning, it does not have an identity – or at least an identity that can be appreciated rationally. Protest may be made that the concept of infinity is rational. I can only reply that it is conjured out of a contrived rationality which has no point of reference or accountability but the mind's own supposed free impetus. It may have philosophical and mathematical *convenience*, and be entirely useful in this way, but therein is its limit.

I am well aware that we have to distinguish (though the distinction is by no means uniformly clear cut and obvious) between formal or symbolic logic and general philosophy, the mathematical and the metaphysical. The formal logician is preoccupied primarily, but not exclusively, with the logic of concepts such as *some*, *all*, *beyond*, *besides*, *if*, *or*, and so on. The more general philosopher concerns himself primarily (but again not exclusively so) with more tangible factors – *seeing*, *hearing*, *perception*, *enjoying*, *comprehending*, *remembering*, for example.

Clearly there is an overlap, but the method of the formal logician is different from that of the general philosopher, for the former, fundamentally, is dealing primarily (but only primarily) with what are theoretical concepts of a mathematical quality, the latter with more tangible concepts.

However, the influence of the former, from the days of Ockham through to Leibniz and later Bertram Russell with the latter two's emphasis on the claim that philosophers would be able to operate ultimately by reducing everything to calculation, and also through to the onrush of logical positivism, now hopefully disparaged, and the present stress on formal logic, has left a distinct mark on philosophical attitudes.

There is still the all-pervading notion, perhaps unconscious but nevertheless determinative, of the autonomy of the mind and that philosophical or mathematical precision and convenience is the door of truth. This may be harsh questioning and the not too precise wielding of a big stick, but the point is that for the systematic theologian the terms *infinity*, *infinite*, as pursued by the philosopher, can be questionable indeed when the mathematical approach is not tempered and made to serve the ontological.

Behind this questioning of philosophy's assumptions in the direction of mathematical logic lies the theological assertion of the double contingency of creation. That is to say that creation is utterly dependent upon God for its existence and its identity – its contingency TO God – and yet it is given by God that identity which is its own nature and mode of existence – its contingency FROM God. The idea of the creation as infinite blurs the distinction (indeed confuses it) between Creator and creature. It is little good saying that it is an infinity with a terminus, namely, as Sorabji above (p. 41) with regard to an infinite past, the present – or our thoughts about the past in the present.

Yet, can we be so evasive and say that it is not the present as such but our thoughts about the past which are in the present? This does not avoid the pressing need for a definition of the present.

But what is the present? It is indefinable and totally elusive, being but the distillation of the future into the past. I have argued this out at length in my previous work, *The Anachronism of Time*, and here merely wish to refer to the problem of time, which is exactly the perplexity of the present. It cannot be used as a measuring point for it has no stability (see pp. 37f above).

The only thing which can be used as such is the mind itself – but not by itself, only in its relation to the realities with which it is confronted. We cannot think unless we have something about which to think, the authority of which lies in its objective integrity.

If objection is made that the past is the objective reality, we must ask, 'but what is the past?' It has gone; it cannot be recalled, grasped, and quantified. It is, for us, insubstantial. It cannot be thought of out of itself, because, for the theologian, time is not created as an entity in and for itself. It is co-created as a product of God creating that which is other than himself. It can only be thought of from the whole objective context of the Creator of all as he confronts us in his self-revelation as he to whom and from whom all temporal and spatial existence is contingent, and who recapitulates in that Word made flesh, all things and therefore all time.

In the process of thinking, the mind, confronted by objective realities, must hold together the realm of the image and the realm of the idea. It has to give place to the verities of the object confronting it and make itself obedient to these. It has to image faithfully that object if it is to perceive the truth about it.

That truth resides in that object, which was what it was before we began thinking about it, is what it is while we are thinking about it, whatever we may think about it, and will be what it is long after we have ceased to think about it. It has its own indwelling integrity. Moreover, it has its self-giving integrity. For it reveals itself as it is in itself. Its inner and its outer integrity are consistent and never contradictory. The role of the mind is to penetrate the outer integrity until the majesty of the inner integrity is laid bare, yet always having awe and respect for that majesty.

But the thoughts called forth by this process – our formulating our ideas about it in statements – have to be referred back constantly to that basic integrity of that object, and reformed again and again in harmony with what it is in itself. Otherwise we depart at a tangent from its essential truth and split the image and the idea. For what we have done is to make a disjunction between our statements about the truth and truth itself as it exists in itself. We then depart into the realms of the indisciplined conjectural.

The concept of *infinity* invites just this. For to what is this concept to be referred? It will be noted in the mathematical/philosophical development of objections to Philoponos outlined above that at various points the argument is sustained only by suppositions summoned in support – even if they are admitted to be suppositions. An imaginary counter of infinity is invoked, as is an infinite way of counting which is conceptually possible in principle (but on what principle does the conception rest and by what verity is it justified, save out of its own logic?)

That is the point. Logic has become a substitute for objective thinking and constant reverification against objective truth. That which was meant to be the handmaid of such clarification has now become the mistress of a theoretical scheme which replaces the economy of contingent realities.

The validity of this substitution founders, I would suggest, on the question of language and terminology. Theology knows that it only has a language conditioned by time and space to deal with the Divine verities. It therefore uses finite terms in a particular way. That is to say, it uses them paradeigmatically (as pointers to) and appropriately (that is in propriety with the object of its study). It does not (or should not) use terms as conclusive and embracing statements.

The object of theological endeavour is the God who is not contained by time or space but who nevertheless bears relation to the created dimension by virtue of his creating it and by his self-revelation as the Word made flesh within the space/time continuum of this existence of ours.

He has revealed himself as the Infinite (but not in the sense that time or space is thought of by some to be infinite: this is an Infinity which is qualitatively different from that supposed infinity) in this world of finitude. It is an Infinity which is radically other than the suggested infinity of the philosopher stressing the mathematical as opposed to the metaphysical.

Theological terms are everyday terms called forth and chosen for their propriety to the self-revelation of God in Christ as he confronts us within the created dimension. But these terms are moulded out of their common usage and refined of their space/time content so that this is not projected into the existence of the God who is not contained by that created dimension, but who rather embraces it in contingent relation to himself.

These terms are (or ought to be) Christologically determined and tested against this source and authority again and again by way of constant reformation. In other words there is a control and an accountability of words and terms against that which gives rise to them and which is objective truth greater than they and of which they are but the witnesses as paradeigmatic and non-embracing statements.

Whatever discipline we pursue, finite language is all that we have – and philosophy is no exception. But what forms philosophical/mathematical language, and to what is it accountable? I would suggest that in the last resort it is only the particular pattern of a logic invented by a particular mind. That does not lead to proper accountability, for it can only be referred to and against such systems of logic. Nor is, as in the sciences, a pattern of language established which is in accord with the range of objects within that particular branch of knowledge.

Perhaps a parallel to this is the fact instanced above that counting infinity must be different from normal counting. I see in this an admission that such a concept as that of this supposed infinity has slipped out of control and has gained its own self-perpetuating existence and mastery, for it must be asked that if appeal is made for an infinite way of counting then equally some sort of infinite language can be the only means of dealing with this concept. Reality has been laid aside.

This is surely further heightened in, for example, Sorabji's point outlined above, that for those who claim a beginningless universe, an infinity of years was always infinite – a completed infinity cannot be achieved by adding to a finite series. How then can any space/time bound terminology, be employed of infinity if, as the expression of this declared issue, the finite cannot achieve the infinite by mere quantity?

Again, what has not been to the forefront in all this deployment of logic, is the fact that the mind is bound and constricted by time and space and cannot burst those limitations. It can point beyond them, but the basis of the propriety of such a paradeigmatic role cannot lie, I would suggest, within the nature and role of any philosophy seeking to deal in abstraction with other than the finite and the temporal.

Such terms as such philosophy employs have no objective reference by which propriety of terminology can be shaped. They can only be referred back again and again to the limited mind from which they arose in the first place.

If the setting out of arguments about infinity on the basis of such logic has any value, it is this; that it lays bare the impossibility of concluding any truth concerning the concept of infinity and including that within any encompassing statement, save to point out the essential elusiveness of any such concept and its final impossibility.

This is amplified by the absurdities of the contradictions which are thrown up by opposing systems of logic, which can only be, in the last resort, proof of the limitations of the mind. As such philosophy's endeavours are a warning to the theologian that the terms 'infinity', 'eternity' and the like, are not to be used in the all too glibly unthinking way which is so prevalent.

Above all, I wish to address a question about the nature and validity of the premises variously assumed by philosophy in regard to any concept of a supposed infinity. Let us return to the issues raised by Zeno of Elea's dialectic expressed in what has been called his paradox, remembering, of course, that the 'paradoxical' argument is double-sided and that we are only dealing with one side. But it is the very nature of that side of the argument which must raise questions as to its propriety, as indeed Zeno so intended.

The way in which there is set out the logical failure of Achilles to overtake the tortoise at a certain point, or the seeming impossibility of us ever reaching a door and going through it, or a loaf of bread never to be absolutely and finally consumed, seems to me to begin at the wrong end of things, so to speak. Because of this, attention is diverted from the real focus of attention – the nature of the race, the journey to the door and the consumption of the loaf of bread. The point of thought's departure about these should be the place where Achilles overtakes the tortoise, the going through the door, the empty plate.

It is evident in all areas of debate concerning an object or an issue that theories are generated under the compulsion of the objectivity of what is being studied and pondered. But these theories only have propriety for the particular matter in hand when they begin by asking the right questions concerning the integrity of the object or problem studied.

All too often the theory is addressed towards a proposition which may not directly be in accord with and attuned to that integrity. To put the matter in its best light, it may be a proposition which is suggested tangentially by the object or problem and really is concerned with another matter altogether. But because emphasis is put on it and it is laboured because it is intriguing, it appears to be addressing the substance of what is in hand, when, in truth, it is unwittingly directed towards another goal and another issue.

There then arise disputes in which the mind is forced to take sides because it appears that we are faced with two contrary claims concerning the truth of that with which we are faced. The logic of each may appear impeccable as each theory is rationally produced step by step. But if the mind is disciplined to let the object reveal itself or the issue unroll itself on its own terms, then it may appreciate that there is a misunderstanding or an entirely mistaken premise in one of the opposing theories which purport to be addressing the same question.

In other words, the wrong question is being asked. It may be the right question when directed towards some other thing or issue, but it has no rapport with what is essential to the matter in hand. Is the paradox of Zeno really a paradox, or is it the deliberate unbalanced statement of one argument about the event of Achilles overtaking the tortoise against an artificial argument only suggested tangentially by that event? This was Zeno's intention.

I must suggest that in so many of the questions asked by some formal logicians overspilling into general philosophy and in so much of the resultant mental endeavour concerning supposed infinity of time and space, if they are not in fact addressing another problem which is slanted away from the real issue. That is to say, they are concerning themselves with the tangential matter of the nature of fractions (a half, a half of a half, a half of a half of a half, and so on) rather than with the factual evidence of the race, the movement to the door, the eating of the loaf.

Simplistically put, perhaps, it is the difference between perceiving one third in totality and wrestling with the suggested problem that one third is .333333333 recurring and never ending. The principal issue is then cloaked and sidetracked. Because we begin from the starting points of Achilles and the tortoise respectively and work towards what is in fact already completed – the overtaking of the latter by the former – an entirely new problem which in fact has nothing to do with the factual event is thrown up and made the main issue.

Nor can this be sidestepped and an attempt made to bring it back on course by talk of potential or actual infinities. The actuality of the event and its nature is solely the determining factor, not a discussion about calculation and, in inseparable harness to this, a usually unconscious attempt to resolve that which lies behind such discussions all the time – the limitations of the human mind.

Robert Grosseteste seems to have grasped this in his observations on infinity. The most succinct treatment of this is found in his *De Luce*, his treatise On Light and the Beginning of Forms. It is to this we will turn later as a theological entrance into the question of the nature of space and the problem of infinity.

4

God and the Language of Space

ONE SIGNIFICANT figure who made an opening for theology to enter and make use of Greek philosophy was the Jewish thinker Philo of Alexandria, c20BC–cAD50. That particular passage through which Christian thought was to enter later and make Greek philosophy its servant rather than its master was his achievement in interweaving Hebraic and Greek thought in a complementary way.

This is seen by the harmonious (though by no means the identical) treatment of the Biblical and Platonic traditions in which he regarded God as utterly transcendent, beyond all that is in creation, every part of and every value and virtue within the created order, yet as the One Who exercises a total and detailed providence in bringing into being, ordering, sustaining and caring for, creation. At the same time, this is also the God of Plato's *Timaeus*, anterior to creation but to whom creation is related necessarily.

There is a rapport between Philo's interpretation of creation and that of Plato in which he uses Platonic concepts to refine and clarify cosmological questions stemming from the Biblical narratives about the relation of the creation to the Creator.

However, while there is this employment of Platonic concepts to serve the Biblical tradition regarding Creator and creation and their relation, there is also a distinction. In Greek fashion Philo thinks through questions assuming a disparity and a gulf between the dimension of the intelligible – the κόσμος νοητός – and the dimension of the sensible – the κόσμος αἰσθητός. That is to say, he operated with a system which distinguished sharply between the spiritual and the physical, the ideal and the real, the 'heavenly' and the 'earthly'. But what distinguishes Philo from merely Greek thought in respect is that the divine is not identified with the dimension of the intelligible, the ideal, the heavenly. Such is his insistence and emphasis on the transcendence of God that God is construed as being above and beyond even the ideal and the intelligible[1]:

> He alone is eternal and the Father of all things intelligible and sensible.

That God is the Creator of ideas as well as the material realities distinguishes Philo from Plato, for whom the ideal was uncreated and eternal[2]. Included in this Philonic category of ideas were the mind and the soul of individual beings, but not, as with Plato, the concept of a cosmic mind and soul, for Philo would not countenance such. This category of ideas is regarded by Philo as being created in the thought of God as the powers by which form and order, rationality and harmony are bestowed upon creation, the sensible or material realities being created secondarily but in correspondence to the ideal.

This raises questions of the relation of time to God, for here something in the mind of God is posited prior, in temporal terms, to the visible and tangible creation. To deal with this question is not our concern here, for it is the relation of God to the ideal upon which I wish to concentrate. The reader may be referred to my observations about creation actualized 'instantaneously' upon the thought of God in chapter 3 of *The Anachronism of Time*, where the difficulties which result from any projection of temporal measurement or content into the existence of God are discussed.

Philo's emphasis here is on the nature of the Logos. For he regarded these ideas as contained in and sustained by the Logos which is also the uncreated Mind and Thought of God. This two-fold aspect of the Logos as the *Idea of ideas*[3] and therefore related to the created rationality of creation as the Container of these ideas archetypal to creation, and yet as the Uncreated and active Mind of God and therefore related to the Uncreated Rationality which God is in Himself, underpins Philo's view of space.

The Logos is the 'place' where the world of ideas, the intelligible, the immaterial created realities, are contained, and, emanating from the Logos, they are the means by which God so orders the whole created reality. Nothing but the Logos could contain the intelligible, the realm of ideas, for the Logos brought them into being, disposing and ordering their sphere.

That there should be a 'place' where ideas reside and from which they come and are given expression and action in relation to the material universe, is intriguing.

This concept of 'space' might best be illustrated with the instance of someone thinking about a scene of, let us say, a sunlit shore with sand and rocks and a forest stretching from its boundaries and rising up into the cliffs and land beyond. This does not occupy 'space' in the literally measurable sense, but the mind is the 'place' of such a place. Or again, a landscape gardener thinking about the proportion and balance and harmonious variety of the area on which he is about to exercise his skill. His envisualizing of the finished scene is there, but does not yet occupy tangible and measurable space. The scene and the completed garden are there in the idea, and that is their 'place' where not only the beginning of the work but the pursuance and completion of it resides.

But the Logos is also the 'place' where we approach the Uncreated and Divine in meeting the Logos without actually reaching the Being of God himself at whose utter transcendence we can never arrive[4]. This is the meeting 'place' of the rationality of the created order with the Rationality which God is in Himself. In other words, Philo perceives the 'place' which the Logos is as the medium of the rational, both the rationality of creation and the active Rationality of God. Space or place here is a matter of relational encounter.

The transcendence of God also underpins Philo's view of space. God is not 'in place', for he is not contained, but contains all[5]. God is beyond 'place' for he is that which brings 'place' into being. He is therefore qualitatively different from anything which has to do with place, for all else other than God is in place. Philo interprets Moses on the mount entering the thick darkness of God's presence not as an entry into a physical state, that is, spatially approaching and meeting God 'in' the cloud, but as the realization of the unapproachableness of God who is beyond all things as the Cause of all.

In the later thought of Pseudo-Dionysius we have a remark-able parallel with this idea of the utter transcendence of God and its attendant language and concepts. God as the *Cause* is also a Pseudo-Dionysian emphasis. In that writer's thought, the Cause is so absolutely transcendent that he is beyond being, space and time. We have, in fact, a line of such ascrip-tion of 'beyondness' to God which runs from Philo through Clement of Alexandria, Origen and Pseudo-Dionysius.

In Clement and Origen and Pseudo-Dionysius there is a treatment of the Logos as the Word made flesh, which has a strong subordinationist tendency in the Word or Son's rela-tion to the Father, and a strong parallel in thought forms to Philonic conceptions (especially in Pseudo-Dionysius) of the Father as the *Cause* and therefore totally beyond our reach. As an aside, this may well be an argument for an Alexandrian origin (and an Origenistic influenced one in particular) for the writings of Pseudo-Dionysius.

Clement develops the thought of Philo, in that God is not regarded as being contained but also that he does not contain the universe. The same sort of position as that taken by Philo had already been stated independently of Alexandrian thought by Hermas[6] who speaks of God as He who:

> has created and fulfilled all things and made them to exist out of non-existence, and contains all things while He himself alone is not contained.

But for Clement, God is absolutely beyond reach with regard to his essential Being, so that He does not even contain creation to which he draws near only by his Power[7]. It is this claim that God does not contain any created dimension which distinguishes Clement from Philo and Hermas. But he does take up Philo's observations on Moses, pointing out that God does not dwell in darkness or space, but is utterly beyond all properties of created things in an ineffable way. In this way, Clement (and Philo before him) corrected the Greek idea of working out the relation between Creator and crea-ture in spatial terms. Clement hardened this by his refutation of the idea of God as a 'container' in any sort of way.

God is therefore perceived in the Clementine writings as being so beyond space and so utterly distinct from it as both

contained by it or containing it, that any approach to the
problem of God's relation to space precludes any existen-
tially related assessment. There is no spatial synthesis even
on the grounds of God containing all that is.

The Clementine emphasis is that space is related to God,
not 'spatially', but as the medium of his power. It is not by
His existence, but by His power that He contains created
realities. With regard to His existence He is distant in a way
that exceeds any measure of space; with regards to His
Power He is very near[8]. This means that we are concerned
with space as the 'place' where we are related to the activity
of God and as the medium in which events occur as a result.

This of course is basically Platonism insofar as there is
present this consideration of space as the formless medium in
which events occur. But space is – and this is the difference to
mere Platonism – the medium where things happen because
it is caused by the relational effect of the created and Uncreated rationalities. This is distinct from the Platonic notion
of space as the arena of the cosmic mind or soul.

But we must ask if there does not lurk behind the idea of
the utter transcendence of God, and the limiting of space as
the arena of only his power and activity, an even more radical dualism than that of Greek thought with its gulf between
the sensible and the intelligible.

It is one thing to say that God is beyond all created being
and another that he is beyond all being as was Origen's wont.
In the last resort for Clement, the incarnation means that
although the Son is described as God and becomes Man, the
primary significance of Christ lies in that He, as the revelation of God, is an activity of the Father, distinct from the
Father, but an activity mainly, and, indeed in the last resort,
it may be suspected, only[9].

Despite such a merely ergonistic interpretation of the relation of the Son to the Father, this had the effect of regarding
the possibility of faith arrived at through Christ within the
dimensions of space and time as anchored in the divine will
of the eternal Father. Clement construed the order of what
the Word or Son does on earth amid the rationalities of the
created dimension as grounded in the eternal order of the
Will of God in His uncreated Rationality, and thereby

strongly emphasised the issue of the relation of the rationality of creation to the divine Rationality of the Creator. The incarnation is not a particular and even unique manifestation of God's activity within created space, but is the expression of the eternal works and words in the divine Will and Being. In this way, created space and immeasurable God are related [10].

We have here, in an undefined fashion, a glimmering of the later thought of the double contingency of creation: that is, that creation is totally dependent upon God for its beginning, dimension, identity and nature, yet it has bestowed upon it precisely that beginning, dimension, identity and nature distinct from God in his uncreated identity and nature. Creation is free to be itself – that is its contingency *from* God – but this can only be in harmony with its dependence upon God – its contingency *to* him. In other words the freedom and rationality of creation is genuine only in its relation to the Freedom and Rationality of God. It is free *for* God and rational in its created correspondence to him.

It is this later concept of double contingency, so emphatically found in the writings of Irenaeus and later Athanasius, which speaks out clearly, if implicitly, about the nature of space.

The consideration entered on here, following the observations above on the absolute transcendence of God, is the use and repercussions of language used to speak of such a God. This is best exemplified in the writings of Pseudo-Dionysius.

At the very beginning of *The Divine Names*, that writer sets out the problem of this transcendence of God and the inability of direct speech to even begin to describe this God. He undertakes his task *as far as is possible* [11].

This possibility does not reside in words of *human wisdom* but in the power of the Holy Spirit. Here more than a note of caution has to be sounded. Given the concept of a God who is beyond all created being how can we speak of such a God since our language is born of and borne with time and space? Such a God is beyond such speech. Are we therefore committed or condemned to utterances which are either unintelligible to normal forms of language – speaking in tongues – or viewing the dimension in which we live and move and have our being as that from which we must seek to escape if we are to have any contact with what lies beyond this measured existence of ours?

Undoubtedly the direction of the thought of Pseudo-Dionysius advocates what has been generally called 'mysticism', as the way of rising to the Divine. In one sense, this 'mysticism' is the theological equivalent of the mathematical/philosophical approach of the philosopher in questions of the Infinite, as opposed to the ontological/philosophical emphasis, in that it involves a forsaking of the temporal/spatial realities as they are in themselves, and a dismissal of the discipline of objective, κατὰ φύσιν, according to nature, thinking.

The ontological and the metaphysical/philosophical approach, on the other hand, as the term 'metaphysical' seems to suggest, might lead equally to a 'mysticism' by way of looking at the objective realities, and discarding them as 'unworthy' – the equivalent of the *via negativa* approach which in some periods of history theology adopted -- nevertheless at least initially taking stock of the created dimension and examining it as it is in itself. This has not led by any means to a disparagement of these temporal/spatial entities in all of the metaphysical approaches. It is in the positive analysis of them and their significance that philosophy does walk hand in hand with theology to their mutual benefit.

Pseudo-Dionysius does, to an extent, deal with the created dimension in its temporal/spatial reality, but such is his idea of the utter transcendence of God, that he flies off into mystical realms aided by a rather simplistic mathematical approach and speculation concerning unity and diversity.

However, having said that, he does wrestle in a profound way with the relation of God to all creation, to space and time. His difficulty is to express the utter distinction between Creator and creation, yet maintain a bond between them. In this he singularly fails. In the last resort, having said so much that is of value of the reality of this relation, particularly where there are hints of a double contingency of creation to and from the Creator[12], he resorts to a 'spiritualizing' and a 'mysticizing' of that relation, denying the validity of any language about God. We are, in his opinion, to forsake

ultimately the bounds of created being and the spatial/
temporal realities.

This can be seen in his view of the place of the Scriptures
as the revelation of God:

> Now as I have said already, we dare not apply words or
> conceptions to this hidden transcendent God. We may only
> use the information of scripture. God has kindly shown us
> that understanding and direct contemplation of Himself is
> impossible for created beings, since He is above all being[13].

Pseudo-Dionysius thereby demonstrates his far from im-
partial use of scripture. It is noteworthy that most of his
quotations are merely to do with the transcendence and
overwhelming majesty of God. The same is true of his
treatment of the Incarnation. While his language dealing
with the Incarnation is couched clearly in terms of the
Council of Chalcedon regarding the union of the two natures
of Christ –

> He has come to unite with us in what we are without himself
> undergoing change or confusion[14] –

nevertheless, Christ is used in an almost Gnostic sense of illuminating and raising up from the created dimension by way
of divinizing the mind to make it fit to receive – not directly,
but through the revelations of the hierarchy of purer and yet
purer spirits – and to perceive the Divine vision.

Indeed, the overall impression is given that Pseudo-
Dionysius operates with a scheme whereby he perceives the
divinization of the mind as the forsaking and forswearing of
all that is tangible and that mind's progress through levels
and stages of enlightenment until it approximates to the eternal Being of God, and into this is fitted the incarnation as the
principle of this scheme, bolstered by a highly selective use of
scripture. If he has not already done so, he is in danger of
approximating to a type of gnosticism based on Neo-
Platonic assumptions. I would go as far as to suggest that for
him, Christianity holds some of the essence of this and is
interpreted accordingly.

Because of this we are faced with a severe dualism as the
outcome of Pseudo-Dionysius's thought. Thus:

My counsel to you in searching for the hidden things, is to forsake everything perceived and understood, everything perceptible and understandable, everything which is and everything which is not, and with your understanding removed to reach above to the best of your ability toward union with him who is above all being and knowledge. Through full and unequivocal abandoning yourself and all things, forsaking all and freed from all, you will be lifted up to the light of the divine shadow which is above all existence.[15]

So too his description of Moses in communion with God on the mount:

He [Moses] breaks free of them, away from that which sees and that which is seen, and rushes into the verily mysterious darkness of unknowing. Here, renouncing all that the mind may understand, enveloped totally in the intangible and the invisible, he belongs utterly to the one who is beyond everything. Here, not oneself or anyone else, one is supremely united by a totally unknown activity of all knowledge, and knows beyond the mind by knowing nothing.[16]

And again, in *The Divine Names* referring to the Deity:

Mind beyond mind, word beyond expression, it is encompassed by no discourse, no intuition, no name.[17]

There is a considerable parallel between Psuedo-Dionysius's *Mystical Theology* and the comments of Gregory of Nazianzen. To read sections 1000C, D and 1001A of the former and compare them with Gregory's *Oration XXVIII: 12, 3*, suggest a strong link of themes. For these works share, in observations about Moses speaking with God on the mount, the same themes of, the necessity of purification and Moses's withdrawal from those who are not so purified, the cloud surrounding God, the withdrawal of Moses from matter and material things, his not actually seeing the Being of God, but His presence.

There are parallels also between Pseudo-Dionysius and Gregory of Nyssa's *Life of Moses*. All these, and the terminology used, would suggest that Pseudo-Dionysius, given a fifth century dating at the earliest, was beholden to the works of Gregory of Nyssa and Gregory of Nazianzen, and to Philo and Clement before them, though he transforms the substance of their argument into flights of what is commonly called 'mysticism' in his eccentric development of their thought. The incarnation, for him, has no central and determinative role.

Gregory of Nazianzen's *Theological Orations* are a source for the 4th century patristic understanding of space and all the issues involved in speaking about space and its relation to the Creator. He, too, emphasises the difficulty of using terminology about God. His warfare against the Eunomians, besides being waged over the question of the interior relations of the Trinity, was concerned also with the problem as to whether or not the Divine nature was totally comprehensible. The Eunomians maintained that it was; Gregory denied this supposition. That is not to say that he took the same line as Pseudo-Dionysius was to adopt later.

At first sight it may appear that his stand is that of the later Pseudo-Dionysius – that God is beyond words[18].

> The Deity cannot be expressed in words. And this is proved to us, not only by arguments, but by the wisest and most ancient of the Hebrews, so far as they have given us reason for conjecture. For they appropriated certain characters to the honour of the Deity, and would not even allow the name of anything inferior to God to be written with the same letters as that of God, because to their mind it was improper that the Deity should even to that extent admit any of His creatures to have a share with Himself. How then could they have admitted that the indivisible and separate nature can be explained by divisible words?

What Gregory is underlining here is that the *how* – the τὸ δέ πῶς – of the eternal and interior existence of God as Father, Son and Holy Spirit, and the eternal begetting of the Son by the Father, is not within the capability of language to describe[19].

> How was He begotten? – I repeat the question in indignation. The begetting of God must be honoured in silence. It is a great thing for you to learn that He was begotten. But the manner of His generation we will not admit that even Angels can conceive, much less you. Shall I tell you how it was? It was in a manner known to the Father Who begat, and to the Son Who was begotten. Anything more than this is hidden by a cloud, and escapes your dim sight.

That this self-same God reveals himself in the incarnation of the Word, is another matter. For, although again it is not permissible to speak of the 'how' of the Incarnation, here it is permissible to speak of God in accordance with the terms in which God so reveals himself in accommodating himself to our limitations. Only God speaks well of God, but God's speaking is heard by us as His Word made flesh in and according to our limitations.

Moreover, our created being is affirmed in its true identity by this union with the Divine. This is very much worked out by Gregory of Nazianzen in terms of the *Royal exchange*, that is, that God assumed our nature and flesh and limitations that we may share in His Divine life. But there is no question of our losing our limitations and essential created dimension. Rather, it is seen to be in Christ what God intended it to be.

The same, therefore, holds true of our thinking and talking about God. The way of so doing with propriety is given in Christ. Our limited terminology is then shown to be in accordance with the eternal and infinite God in the sense that it becomes, in Christ, an appropriate pointer to Him. It still is limited and temporal and spatial terminology, but it is opened out to that which lies beyond it, which words cannot encompass or thoughts circumscribe[20].

But under the compulsion of the objective fact of the Person and event of Jesus Christ, the Word made flesh, it is endowed with a paradeigmatic nature, and bent out of its solely creaturely reference, it is affirmed as appropriate speech about God. Herein lies the propriety and therefore the possibility of theological language. Thus herein is the propriety and possibility of speaking about that which is beyond all created being and thought, for it speaks out of that centre which is God Himself, the Word Incarnate. This enables it to have an sufficient, articulate grasp of the knowledge of the One who is eternal and infinite in the language of the temporal and the spatial, without subsuming Him arrogantly within the limitations of that dimension which that One has made His own while remaining Lord over it.

This is far removed from the direction in which Pseudo-Dionysius was later to head, with rather unfortunate consequences for the thought of the Middle Ages which he, in certain quarters and particularly in the west, influenced. This led, I would suggest, to the beginning of the forsaking of any attempt to follow through the patristic attempt to deal with the infinity of God and His relation to space and time, making it all too easy for there to be a substitution of a 'mysticism' and a 'spirituality' for rational theological, and particularly Christological, endeavour, in bridging the distinction between Creator and creature and coming to terms with that relation – an all too contemporary phenomenon.

Behind all this lies the acknowledgement that we cannot know God from His works – that is, creation – for we speak looking down into the depths of the infinite distance which separates Creator from creature. What is not acknowledged is that all our philosophy can only echo pointlessly and fade away in that chasm, for it is in that depth that 'mysticism' and 'spirituality' are conceived in desperation and too often mistake their direction and think that they are rising to higher spheres. All too often this is seen by practitioners in other disciplines as theology's capitulation before the demands of rationality.

There is also, of course, an equally abortive attempt to step over that infinite gulf by what is commonly known as 'Natural Theology', which, in this common instance means reading the nature of God from the appearance of nature. This, however, is noted for its singular way of choosing only the 'beautiful' and the acceptable in nature to achieve this. It does not address itself to that nature red in tooth and claw, that nature of the cataclysm and the disaster.

This also rests on a fundamental dualism, between nature as it really is in its totality (most of which is conveniently and romantically ignored) and the Creator as He exists in the indescribable majesty of the mystery of his eternal Being. It depends on a dualism between form and content; for it seems, for example in such attitudes, to be acceptable to see God in the beauty of the autumnal colours but ignore the fact that these hues are distilled by the alchemy of death; or, again, to eulogise the sweetness of the sound of God's feathered creatures, proving the existence of a tender Creator, while being oblivious to the fact that bird song is more often a matter of aggressive assertiveness and territorial jealousy. It consists of a crude idealization of form and an ignorant refusal to consider content.

But such shallow piety and narrow theology need not detain us. Neither it nor any 'mysticism' or 'spirituality' address the problem of God and His relation to space – and, indeed, arise because they side-step that issue. Suffice it to say here in passing that there is indeed a perfectly arguable natural theology, but one found only by looking at creation through the Person, fact and event of the Word made flesh, the Creator of all in the midst of His own handiwork, and the question of revelation in incarnation, suffering, crucifixion, resurrection and ascension which that entails. For here, theology would maintain, the 'place' and 'space' of God takes into itself the 'place' and 'space' of creation.

Whenever Christology is displaced as the centre and controlling factor in all our thoughts about God, then the mind strays. Even when the doctrine of the Person of Christ, and therefore the Self-revelation of God is given place, there is still the danger of the vagaries of the mind floating where they will. This is because faith, which is our 'amen' to all that Christology implies, finds itself faced with, on the one hand, the compelling objectivity of God's truth in Christ, and on the other that this truth opens out to the full mystery and unencompassed Being of God. The temptation is to pay lip service to the former and not let it be the directive towards that fulness of God on its own terms. Opinions then become elevated to the status of dogmas, and Christ has been used as a means to another end.

What we are concerned about in that Self-revelation of God is not just the objective knowledge which the Person, fact and event of Jesus Christ gives, but a sharing in the knowledge which God has of Himself. This is the substance of the faith. God in his Self-revelation is not an object to be viewed dispassionately and disinterestedly. It is his Self-giving in which we are given to participate in the knowledge the Father has of the Son and the Son of the Father in the mutual bond of Divine love which is the Holy Spirit. But this is governed strictly by the nature of that Self-revelation. This is why the doctrine of the Trinity of God is immediate on the doctrine of the Person of Christ.

Gregory of Nazianzen outlines the contradictions into which we fall if we look for God and the things of God only with what he calls the *approximations of reason*[21].

> For what will you conceive the Deity to be, if you rely upon all the approximations of reason? Or to what will reason carry you, O most philosophic of men and best of Theologians, who boast of your familiarity with the Unlimited.

In other words, if we start off with ideas about infinity or eternity or boundlessness, incorporeality and so on, on the basis only of the scrutiny of reasoning, then we will fall into absurd contradictions.

These he sets out, first[22] showing the contradictions in the arguments about the Deity being corporeal, which totally dispenses with his divinity and confuses the distinction between Creator and creature. Nor could there be any Aristotelian suggestion that God is immaterial and a *Fifth Element*, a formless matter carried round in a circular movement and moving all things below it. For what, asks Gregory moves that, and what moves the mover of that? If God is subject to motion, even if he is immaterial, how can he help being contained in space?

He points out that the whole question of the corporeality or incorporeality of God on any philosophic basis is absurd. For if such an approach deems God alone to be incorporeal, what of the angels which minister to him? Do they have bodies, or, are they of the same incorporeal nature as he, and how then is he superior to them? Gregory is really asking if this argument does not depend on positing measures of incorporeality, and if this in fact does not presume corporeal qualities.

> And if He is above them [the angels], there is brought in an irrational swarm of bodies, and a depth of nonsense, that has no possible basis to stand on.

The limitations of using such philosophic terms as *Incorporeal* are then set out. Gregory has this stricture to make: that God is certainly not corporeal, and therefore he must be construed as incorporeal.

> But this term Incorporeal, though granted, does not yet set
> before us – or contain within itself His Essence, or any more
> than Unbegotten, or Unoriginate, or Unchanging, or
> Incorruptible, or any other predicate which is used concerning
> God or in reference to Him.

It is only those who have the mind of God who can speak
with any propriety and fulness, as far as humanity is able,
about God. This phrase *who have the mind of God* refers to
the theological discipline of letting the Self-revelation of God
confront and inform the mind on God's own terms. Here,
Gregory echoes Athanasius in the matter of philosophical
language over against theological language[23]:

> It would be more godly and true to signify God from the Son
> and call him Father, than to name God from his works alone
> and call him Unoriginate.

What lies behind this are the vastly different approaches
taken respectively by philosophy and theology. The philosophy which Gregory Nazianzen and Athanasius were questioning dealt in concepts in their relation to created entities –
either positively or negatively, and if the latter still relative to
the created dimension – and produced theoretical frame-
works of relational thought; theology, on the other hand,
deals not with theoretical or conceptual attitudes, but with
relational existences as they are dynamically revealed.

That is to say, the basis of the fourth century Nicene theology was the relation of the Father and the Son in the bond of
divine love the Holy Spirit, as revealed in that Son or Word
as flesh and human nature. The difference is that between the
Creator/creation relation and the Father/Son relation.

Athanasius emphasised that to approach God as Father
through the Son is more rational and accurate, since the Son
is the Self-revelation of God whereby we have entrance into
the knowledge which God has of himself as he exists as the
Triune God, than to attempt to discover the Creator in any
way through the created realities by deduction.

Behind this is the distinction between describing with
conceptual terms what are essentially static constructions,
and a dynamic and living existence with terms appropriate to
its nature. The difficulty that theology faces is that all that is

available in some respects are static terms to describe dynamic situations. That is why it has to be careful – literally 'full of care' for its choice of terminology, the reasons it must give for that choice, and the reasons it must give as to how it is applying what is so chosen.

It is within the given framework of the Self-revelation of God, and the dynamic sphere which that opens up, that theology may legitimately turn to philosophical concepts for assistance and clarification in fulfilling its work. But it will endow these concepts with a dynamic aim in all propriety for the nature of the God who is as he acts and acts as he is.

At no point will theology think that, however sharply it has clarified its terminology and however profoundly it has deepened its concepts, it has adequately described that God. We may turn again to Gregory of Nazianzen who illustrates (and philosophers might excuse what they deem to be intemperate language) what happens when we indulge in discourses and concepts by which the mind[24]

> despises noble simplicity, and has introduced a crooked and intricate style.

In fairness to philosophy, he is criticizing the ostentatious dialectics of Aetius and Eunomius – but a warning of a general kind is there.

Having spoken of the incorporeality of God, he goes on to write[25]:

> Is He Nowhere or Somewhere? For if He is Nowhere, then some person of a very inquiring turn of mind might ask, How is it then that He can even exist? For if the non-existent is nowhere, then that which is nowhere is also perhaps non-existent. But if He is Somewhere, He must be either in the Universe, or above the Universe. And if He is in the Universe, then He must be either in some part or in the whole. If in some part, then He will be circumscribed by that part which is less than Himself; but if everywhere, then by one which is further and greater – I mean the Universal, which contains the Particular; if the Universe is to be contained by the Universe, and no place is to be free from circumscription. This follows if He is contained in the Universe. And besides, where was He before the Universe was created? for this is a point of no little difficulty. But if He is above the Universe, is there nothing to distinguish this from the Universe, and where is this above

situated? And how could this Transcendence and that which is transcended be distinguished in thought, if there is not a limit to divide and define them? Is it not necessary that there should be some mean to mark off the Universe from that which is above the Universe? And what could this be but Place, which we have already rejected? For I have not yet brought forward the point that God would be altogether circumscript, if He were even comprehensible in thought: for comprehension is one form of circumscription.

If the relation between God and space is to be examined and discussed, then measurement, mathematical quantity, if this be the approach adopted, can only lead to contradiction and absurdity. Equally, the transcendence of God cannot be of such a quality that he is construed as being beyond being itself. For then there would be no relation and we are equally faced with the absurdity of the attempt to relate to God through the abandonment of all reason and the eventual rejection of all created things.

But, it has been underlined, we need to examine closely the way that terms are to be used dynamically in order to try to speak of a relation between God and space. This will involve us in a rejection of the idea that God is space writ large, or even infinite space – for he is then not qualitatively different from His creation, as Gregory of Nazianzen makes clear. Nor will it do to look at space in Platonic terms as the formless medium where events happen. That may be approximating to part of the truth, but it confines the interaction of God with space to the power of God, in terms of Clement of Alexandria's understanding, and excludes God's being. This, too, means that in the last resort there is no relation of the existence of the Creator to the existence of creation.

We turn to look at this question – not, conceptually, by trying to work out the relation between the Infinite and the finite – but by reversing the commonly practised process and putting spatial conceptions of *nearness* and *farness*, *remoteness* and *proximity*, under the scrutiny of that central, determinative doctrine of the Person of Christ, where God and human being are united, and interpreting them in that light.

5

The Trinity, the Incarnation and Space

THE OMNIPRESENCE of God is an expression of his freedom. It is the particular declaration that he is not excluded from any area of existence. The omnipotence of God is likewise such an affirmation of his freedom. It is the particular declaration that he is not limited in any sphere of ability.

However, both the omnipresence and the omnipotence of God, as expressions, require a careful approach in an attempt to understand them. He is not omnipresent in the sense that he is spread out everywhere. Nor is he omnipotent in the way in which power, as we perceive it in the created realities, may be extended to an infinite degree.

The primary requirement of propriety of approach, and thus basic understanding, lies behind such attributes of God, and coalesces in the question of what is meant by the 'freedom' of God.

Freedom means sovereignty, in the sense that God is free to be the God he is, and therefore free to create. For in his freedom he has declared himself to be the Creator God. Nothing exists without him. All that is can only exist and have its own presence because it depends on the existence and presence of God. Nothing exists without him, yet it exists in its own sphere and with its own identity, which is not the sphere or the identity of God. This is a statement of the double contingency of creation; that all things are contingent TO God, for they totally depend upon him as Creator for their being and presence, yet they are contingent FROM him, for they are created with an identity and a presence distinct from God. They are created and he is uncreated.

The relation between the created and the uncreated is of basic importance in any understanding of the nature of creation and of the freedom of the Creator. It is formative, determinative and conclusive of that understanding. This is, of course, a theological statement, but not a view which is incompatible with other disciplines in the fields of scientific endeavour exploring and discussing creation from within its own reality and presence and attempting to find a unitary view which makes sense of all its interwoven facets of order and chaos.

The vantage point on which theology takes its stands is that which may permit such a unitary view on the basis of the self-revelation of God, which is the Word by Whom all things were created and in Whom they consist, made flesh.

This double contingency implies both the nearness and the farness of God – his proximity and yet his distance. From the outset, it must be clear that these are not quantities of space which are measurable. They refer in the first instance to qualitative and relational considerations.

God's remoteness consists in the fact that he is not created, but is totally Other. This statement cannot, however, stand by itself. As noted above, Gregory Nazianzen pointedly broke the validity of any such *via negativa* approach to an understanding of God[1], that God is not mortal, not frail, not limited by what is called time and space, and so on – even if it has resurfaced at intervals in Christian thought.

> But a man who states what God is not, without going on to say what He is, acts in much the same way as one would who when asked how many twice five make, should answer 'Not two, nor three, nor four, nor five, nor twenty, nor thirty, nor in short any number below ten or any multiple of ten'; but would not answer 'ten', nor settle the mind of his questioner upon the firm ground of his answer. For it is much easier, and more concise to show what a thing is not from what it is, than to demonstrate what it is by stripping it of what it is not.

We cannot know what God is not if we do not know what he is. This is where the assertion of God's proximity has to be considered primarily.

God is near to creation in his Word. That Word became incarnate. That is, the Creator took that which makes creation what it is, to himself. More properly stated, this means that the Creator brings creation into proximity with himself. There we see what God is, and in that closeness in which the created realities are not swallowed up in the uncreated presence of the Creator, but are affirmed in their identity and nature, and in which the uncreated reality of God is not diminished or compromised or changed, then we may see what God is not.

This is why the doctrine of the Person of Christ, the incarnate Word, is determinative of all theological thought in this matter of the relation of creation to Creator and in the question of the freedom of God. It is of fundamental necessity that the mode of the incarnation be held as an entrance into any theological discussion in this area.

We are concerned here with the statement that God in all his 'Godness' – and nothing less than God without change or diminution – took to himself our humanity, all that goes to make up what we are in the reality of our frailty and mortality – and not some idealized or symbolic flesh and nature – and gave that particular humanity existence and presence as the man Jesus Christ. This is the union of the Divine and human natures in the incarnation. It is a union, not a mixture or a loose conjunction, in which the reality of both natures is affirmed in the one Jesus Christ. There is no aspect of the human nature missing. What is termed 'mind,' 'body' and 'soul', is given existence from the moment of conception by the Blessed Virgin Mary – there is no question of God adopting a good man already living. The humanity of Christ has being and presence only within its union with the being and presence of the eternal Word. It does not exist outside that union.

Here there is a unique contingency TO and contingency FROM, on which an appreciation of the significance of all other contingency depends. The humanity has no existence of its own apart from the Word, yet it has individuality, identity and presence in that union. Although it is in all respects our humanity, yet it is unique humanity in that it is the humanity of God the Creator, to which not only all humanity but all creation is related in this union.

The question of space and the incarnation arose in acute form in the early 17th century in a dispute over Christology between the Lutherans and the Calvinists. But behind this dispute lay a hinterland of questioning about God and physical space which long lingered in partial resolution.

These questions were twofold: first, the question of the nature of God in his interior relations as Father, Son and Holy Spirit, and second the question of God in His exterior acts, centring in this instance on the incarnation and the relation of the nature of the Word to the nature of the humanity of Christ.

1. *Space and Trinity*. Bearing in mind that we cannot say what God is not unless we know what he is, we may embark on the doctrine of the Trinity of God positively by approaching the knowledge of God only by way of God's Self-revelation in Christ. Here in the Word made flesh was not only the entrance to, but also the fulness of, that knowledge. This Athanasius saw with clarity. The Deity of the Son is the Deity of the Father, though in this indivisibility, both are distinct[2]. The same is so of the Spirit. Athanasius sums up his Trinitarian doctrine[3]:

> There is one Form [εἶδος] of Godhead, which is also in the Word; and one God the Father, existing in Himself as He transcends all things, and manifest in the Son as He pervades all things, and in the Spirit as in Him He acts in all things through the Word.

This is why the Nicene fathers insisted in the formulation of the Creed of Nicaea in AD325 that the phrase ὁμοούσιον – of one substance – while not explicitly biblical, yet summing up the essence of the biblical witness, was to be used to describe the relation between Father and Son. The ὁμοούσιον of the Spirit was also implicit and made explicit later that century. Father, Son and Holy Spirit share *one form of Godhead* – that is 'Godness', in the unity of God, yet are distinct Persons, so that God exists not as a barren and sterile and isolated One, but as One Who is diverse and rich in his unity which is a Triunity.

The so-called Athanasian Creed, the origin and history of which is discussed so admirably by J. N. D. Kelly in his *The Athanasian Creed*[4], expands on the doctrine of the Trinity. The section which is significant for our purposes here is[5]:

Qualis Pater, talis Filius, talis et Spiritus sanctus. Increatus Pater, Increatus Filius, increatus Spiritus sanctus: inmensus Pater, inmensus Filius, inmensus Spiritus sanctus; aeternus Pater, aeternus Filius, aeternus Spiritus sanctus; et tamen non tres aeterni sed unus aeternus; sicut non tres increati nec tres inmensi, sed unus increatus et unus inmensus. Similiter omnipotens Pater, omnipotens Filius, omnipotens Spiritus sanctus, et tamen non tres omnipotentes, sed unus omnipotens.

Such as the Father is, such is the Son, such also the Holy Spirit. The Father is increate, the Son increate, the Holy Spirit increate. The Father is infinite, the Son infinite, the Holy Spirit infinite. The Father is eternal, the Son eternal, the Holy Spirit eternal. Yet there are not three eternals, but one eternal; just as there are not three increates or three infinites, but one increate and one infinite. In the same way, the Father is almightly, the Son almighty, the Holy Spirit almighty; yet there are not three almighties, but one almighty.

Whatever the origin and earliest date of this Creed, this section has as a hinterland the concern in the Church, made immediate by the necessity of combating the Arian heresy in the fourth century, concerning the complex difficulty of attempting to describe God's nature in terms of his relation to space and time.

What is of note for our purposes in this section is the juxtaposition in sequence of *increatus, inmensus, aeternus, omnipotens.*

Inmensus is translated *infinite* in the form cited by J. N. D. Kelly. The Prayer Book version translates it as *incomprehensible*. What is of significance here is not the confine of a particular translation, but that to which the word itself points. That is more than can be comprehended and fully designated by the limitation of words. Indeed, both translations signify suitably, but partially, in their diverse ways to that which they strive to describe.

The root *men* of the Latin term implies both 'mind' and 'measurement'. That both are incapable of any adequacy in an attempt towards a suitable description of God is the purpose of the term *inmensus*. But there is a more radical concern which the happy conjunction of these terms headed by *increatus* leads though it may not have been explicitly present in the intent of author or translators.

Increatus points to the being of God as utterly qualitatively distinct from the existence of creatures, their attributes and limitations. This is the head in which all the other terms are contained and of which they are but partial comments.

The creature cannot imagine the uncreated source of all being, for it is limited by its creaturely dimensions and out of these it cannot burst. It is not a question of enlarging what we already know to the *nth* degree and calling that God, of projecting concepts and values to what we think is an infinity and perceiving God to be equal to this. The subject of infinity has been entered upon earlier, but suffice it here to note Robert Grosseteste's observation in the 13th century that all our vaunted infinities are but finite to God[6].

> For just as those things which in fact are finite in themselves, and to us are infinite, so things which in fact are infinite in themselves are finite to Him.

The failure which is commonly seen is that of equating the disparity of smallness of quantity and vastness of quantity with differential of quality. So ingrained is this way of thinking that the radical difference is not appreciated. This is why the translation *infinite* is of itself unsatisfactory. *Incomprehensible* goes some of the way to rectifying that, but it must not be seen as totally negative – that it is impossible for the mind to grapple with the thoughts of God. It is rather a warning that God cannot be dealt with in ways in which created objects, which by their very nature are dimensionally compatible to the workings of our minds in their created limitations, are scrutinized and debated. The measurements of the created dimension are not applicable to God. Nor are the workings of the mind as applied to realities within this dimension proper to the verities of God. Athanasius in the 4th century expands and clarifies[7] Isaiah's observation that God is beyond comparison into a necessary dictum standing at the head of all theological endeavour.

This raises the question as to whether or not we can say anything at all about God, theology being but a *via negativa*. But again, to emphasise what has been mentioned already, Gregory Nazianzen points out[8], we cannot say what God is not unless we know what he is.

The logic of that is beyond dispute if we think carefully. The two initial negative adjectives are not the sum and substance of the Athanasian Creed. Rather they are clearing the way for the mind to think in terms appropriate to God, that is, for the mind to adjust to the fact that God reveals himself on His own terms. This Self-revelation of God is set out in the latter part of that Creed in the section on the incarnation of the Word.

We are left with the conclusion that just as 'infinity' is a comment on the limitations of the human mind, baffled even in the last resort by ultimate truths within the created dimension, so too, these adjectives are like comments and warnings on the operation of the mind when dealing with the things of God rather than assertions about God primarily. They are, like all verbal images, convenient for humanity (in this case, the convenience of exhortation about methodological procedure) rather than suitable for God.

The same has to be said of the two remaining seemingly positive adjectives *aeternus* and *omnipotens*. What we call 'eternal' is sometimes described as 'timeless'. This by itself is a meaningless term, so totally negative that it leads to no positive value whatsoever. Nor can 'eternal' be described as it is variously as 'time without end'. That is merely to project vastness of created measurement into God. We cannot even deal adequately with the concept of what we call 'time', and, indeed, constantly confuse its measurement with a supposed quality. Its divisions of convenience into 'past', 'present' and 'future', do not bear analysis when we ask what these in actuality are. The past has gone, the future (if there be one – and that cannot be taken for granted) is not yet, and what is the 'present'? The last is so infinitesimal that it cannot be measured. Yet time is a dimension of creation. What we are really talking about when we speak of time is the quality of created existence as it expresses itself – not measurement of quantity[9]. Time has no substance apart from existence. It is not a created entity, but co-created as an attribute of the mode of created existence. It is, of course, profoundly bracketed with space, both concepts of what we call time and space seen to be converging, or rather, taking their source from, existence. This has to be enlarged upon later.

The adjective really points to the qualitative distinction between the existence of God as Creator Who is in his Word personalising Person and creature brought into being by that Word as personalised person. There is an utter distinction in quality between them, yet a relation. We are here again in the realm of double contingency. Created existence is contingent TO God, as it is totally dependent on him as the author and orderer of created being, yet contingent FROM God in that created being is given by him an identity, peculiar to itself. It is in the balance of this double contingency that created existence has the integrity of its identity. Yet even that identity of created existence is in correspondence to the Identity of God in His uncreated existence. It is this distinction and correspondence together which command the entrance to an exploration of the concepts of time and space.

The same method applies to a consideration of *omnipotens*. 'Almighty' as applied to God does not mean power as we know it in this created dimension extended to its absolute. What we ultimately know of power is naked force. That is carelessly extended to interpret the term 'Almighty', with disastrous consequences for an understanding of the acts of God and the mode of his working. It inevitably leads to the question 'Why does God not do such and such?', or 'Why does God permit this and that?' Rather, the term 'Almighty' implies that all force in this created dimension, however awesome, is contained and controlled by the power of God which does not express itself in the same way as this force. It is not quantitively greater; it is qualitatively other, and in that lies its potency. God's ways are not our ways, nor his thoughts our thoughts. It is in this light that St Paul's observations[10]: are to be understood.

> The weakness of God is stronger than men ... God hath chosen the weak things of the world to confound the things which are mighty.

In the same way, the power of Christ's death with its necessary attendant symbol of the Cross, is that by which the might of God is 'Almightiness' and qualitatively other than what we know of all powers that be. As such it is 'greater' than, and is the vanquisher of, any other power. The point of the crucifixion is its relation to the creative act of bringing existence into being out of nothing, but also of determining the quality of that being – that is, that creation is held in its very nature against all annihilation and has a fulfilment in that which gave it existence. This fulfilment is not found in the spatial and temporal unfolding of its reality, but in the gathering up of these in ultimate meaning in God. In this fulfilment, the 'last day', the 'judgment', the 'second coming', do not form an event within the spatial and temporal measurements of created existence, but consist of the gathering up of all time and space. The Psalmist's symbolic language, cited in the Epistle to the Hebrews, is pertinent here in describing the acts of God [11]:

> Thou, Lord, didst found the earth in the beginning,
> and the heavens are the work of thy hands;
> they will perish, but thou remainest;
> they will all grow old like a garment,
> like a mantle thou wilt roll them up,
> and they will be changed.
> But thou art the same ...

Space, like time, is subject to the fact that it is comprehended in its totality instantly by God. That is his relation to it.

It follows that God cannot be described, in any of his attributes, by the literal application of terms culled from the created dimension. Nor can he be described by the negation of spatial and temporal realities. To say what God is not by way of odious comparison with what we are or what creation is, is still to use spatial and temporal terms as a measure. Neither positive nor negative use of such terms is propriety of approach. In terms of space, size and place are not applicable to him. Neither is their mere negation. He is qualitatively and utterly other than these, both positively and negatively. Yet, what they are and what they are not have a profound relation to him, declared both in creation and incarnation.

Creation and incarnation are the two sides of the one act of God [12]. All time is of necessity present to God instantly, otherwise he is contingent on time and we can only regard him as existing in terms of infinite time. This can only lead to three-dimensional absurdities in speaking about God and

time. These absurdities are applicable equally when we
consider the issues of God and space.

Nowhere is this more obvious than in the portrayal of the
Trinity by some artists in all ages. To depict God as three
manikins, Father, Son and Holy Spirit, is merely to project
the spatial values of isolated individualism into God. Such
crudely inept symbolism is not helpful towards any understanding of the Triunity of God and what this implies for our
necessitously but necessary partial thinking, understanding
and speaking of God as he exists in himself.

In St John's Gospel we have this Triunity of God tantalis-
ingly set out in the evangelist's treatment of the words of
Christ. The stress in this Gospel, complemented by the three
other Gospels in their distinctive emphases and ways, on the
oneness of the Father and the Son, the nature and role of the
Holy Spirit sent by the Father and bearing the truth of all
that the Son has said and done sets out an entrance into God
as he exists as God. This has been taken seriously as a
source, as revelation creating that evangelist's insight and
contribution.

The oneness of Father, Son and Holy Spirit, yet their
distinctiveness as three Persons, is the distillation of such
scriptural assertions in the early church's proclamation of the
faith, as expressed in its concilear decrees and creeds.

It is not the purpose here to argue out the complex nature
of the Gospels and their relation to each other, but rather
only to pick up what the early church took from these writings, which it regarded as its authoritative sources and the
manner in which it employed them. It is also the purpose to
go on from there and suggest to what this endeavour of the
early church pointed and to what we may further point in the
same disciplined way, with a regard to the integrity of the
process which is involved – namely that God reveals himself
on his own terms and that this prime (and indeed only)
controlling factor is the mode for us, as it was for the early
Church, of interpreting scripture as our source of the
knowledge of God.

The Trinitarian doctrine of the Church sought to express,
in as far as human terms would allow, the existence of God
as he is in himself. That *what God is towards creation and*

us in Jesus Christ, he is in himself, is a dictum we should adopt in this endeavour. The fulness of revelation in Christ, that is, here in Christ is God in all the integrity of his Godness as man, is the beginning, the undistracted and committed course, and the ending of theological endeavour, if theology is to have any credence and value as the science it ought to be.

The early Church struggled with this problem of avoiding the projection of created quantities into God in its terminology. It spoke of the Trinity in terms of the Father 'enveloping, embracing, making room for' the Son; the Son *making room for* the Father; and both *making room for* the Holy Spirit Who in turn *makes room* for the other two. By this it clearly did not mean that there was a jostling for position on the heavenly throne! The Greek term it employed, out of which came the meaning and nuance *enveloping, making room for* – περιχώρησις – was emptied of its spatial connotations. Rather it was more properly construed as *abiding with* or *indwelling*, the one Person of the Trinity resting and abiding in the others. The distinctiveness of each Person is not swallowed up in the others, but such is the nature of each that there is full accord in and with the others. The oneness of the Son and the Father and the Holy Spirit does not change, devalue, compromise or consume the integrity of each. Rather, they exist in their respective integrities in this indwelling.

Here *place* takes on a dynamic interpretation because it is identified with the nature of the Persons of the Trinity. Such is the nature of the Father that he is not without the Son, and such is the nature of both that They are not without the Spirit or the Spirit without the Father and the Son. *Place* becomes an interpretation on the mode of indwelling of the Persons and therefore of the nature of the Triune God. Clearly, *place* is emptied of its normal connotations when we use the term in this way, for it is referring not to created *place* and the spatial measurement which of necessity in this application accompanies it, but to the existence of God to Whom the standards and expectations of temporal and spatial measurement within this created order do not apply. Rather it refers to the dynamic existence of the inherent and internal relations within the Triunity of God – his 'eternal' mode of Being.

This is highlighted when it is said that God is 'far' or 'near'. Indeed various Biblical utterances, for example in the Psalms, would suggest that God is both distant and proximate. Taken by itself, such language seems to imply that spatial measurement is applicable here. But such is only of propriety when the maxim that *what God is in himself he is towards us in Jesus Christ* is borne in mind. Is it the case that God can only be 'proximate' and 'remote' towards creation and humanity if he be these in himself?

It may be argued that such terms are only applicable in the relationship – far or near – of God and creation. But the theology of the 4th century Church, certainly, would consider this by saying that God cannot be of one quality towards us and another quality in himself. If God be not consistent in quality then he is not the God of Whom it is said that there is[13]

no variableness neither shadow of turning.

What then is meant by what seems to be the logical statement which must follow on from the 4th century stricture, namely that we are driven to admit that God is both remoteness and proximity in himself? It may be that he is both remote and near to his creation, and seem so on differing occasions to man. But, again, what he is in his relation to creation can only be the outward manifestation of his essential Being, the sort of God he is. There can be no disjunction. But yet again, may we really apply such terms to the 'eternal' Being of God? Karl Barth make the point and does so[14].

There does exist in Him the wealth of His attributes. But above all there exists in the very unity of this wealth of His the triunity of His essence. Thus there exists a divine proximity and remoteness, real in Him from all eternity, as the basis and presupposition of the essence and existence of creation, and therefore of created proximity and remoteness.

It seems that Barth is applying *remoteness* and *proximity* as attributes of the triune existence of God. Yet it is all very well for him to say that God is present to himself (that is in the diversity of Persons), that he not only exists but is co-existent, and that co-existence with *another* (that is, creation), granted by him, is

> no contradiction to His essence. On the contrary, it corresponds to it.

But if he means that there is a direct analogy within the Trinity to created remoteness and proximity in the way things exist in relation to one another in this created dimension, then he is guilty of a simplistic application of an *analogia entis*.

In all that follows this statement, Barth does not bring that out and clarify it, but speaks of the relation of God to creation in terms of God's love and omnipresence. He had previously stated that this omnipresence is the external manifestation and realisation of what God is in himself, but the basis of that omnipresence is the fact that there is in himself[15]

> proximity and remoteness in irresolvable unity

and that in this divine unity

> there is no proximity without remoteness and remoteness without proximity.

This contrasts with the created dimension where there is no such unity, but

> proximity apart from remoteness and remoteness apart from proximity.

There is therefore the acknowledgement that there is an *analogia creationis*. But the assertion (and the very use of the terms) that there is proximity and remoteness in the existence of God as he is in himself, is not saved from confusion by Barth's prior statement. Had he gone on to say that the relationship between proximity and remoteness, namely their union, such as is not found in the created dimension, precludes the use of these terms, carrying as they do too clear an echo of their created incompatibility, and that perhaps the analogy is better served by seeing it in terms of God's Oneness as the unity in diversity of the Three Persons, and that this diversity in unity is reflected in creaturely fashion in the proximity yet remoteness of created beings, then resolution might have been clearer. As it is, his use of these terms only heightens the suspicion that *remoteness*, even in unity with *proximity* in God, points to a latent subordination of the Son, and indeed the Spirit, to the Father in Barth's wider thought and works.

Propriety of terms is of paramount importance if language is to be used as the appropriate pointer to the Self-revelation of God. It is no good applying terms and pleading for their use by the device of claiming that their relationship vis-a-vis God is distinct and other than how they are found in the created dimension. This is a covert *via negativa*.

No doubt Barth's conscious aim is far from this, but the rather misty route of his argument suggests that he has not cleared the air with regard to the basic problem of space and God, and, that despite all that he draws out so admirably later on, there is still an irresolute groping at the heart of the matter. His acceptance and use (though not unqualified, but dealt with in much the same manner as his use of *proximity* and *remoteness*) of the terms *timeless, spaceless,* and *infinite* do not dispel questions of his irresolution of the matter of the fundamental relation of God as he exists in himself to the created realities which He has brought into being. In this respect perhaps he forsook too much the dialectic emphasis (exaggerated as it may have been) of his Commentary on Romans, and became too blandly dialogical.

Remoteness and *proximity* are terms applicable only to the created order. Even to say that God is remote from or near to creation presupposes that he is in some way measurable, or that the 'place' of God can be moveably nearer or farther in relation to created 'place'. The use of the terms suggests that we have not rid ourselves of secretly transferring created values of measurements and dimensions into God.

The better way is via a terminology which is not connected with measurement only, but, even if some hint of measurement is involved, refers primarily to quality of existence.

It has already been indicated than when speaking of the Triune existence of God, we are speaking of relational 'measurement', the Personal relation between Father, Son and Holy Spirit. The 'place' of each, the 'space' each possesses, is not quantitative, but qualitative and this in an ineffable way – not comparable with any existence that we know within this created dimension in which we live, move and have our being as well as our place and space.

We are therefore concerned with relational questions rather than quantitive measurements. The relations of God to creation and creation to God are to be treated likewise. This is laid out more immediately in the second consideration, the relation of the nature of the Word to the nature of the humanity he assumed in the Incarnation.

2. *Space and the Word made flesh.* Here the question of the relation of God to created space and place is heightened, for we are concerned with the actuality of God's Being in his Word taking the realities of creation to himself in Incarnation and confronting these realities from within as the man Jesus of Nazareth.

The problem which arose in the 17th century in the dispute as to the mode of the Word assuming flesh – that is humanity in its totality and in its real estate – revolved around the question of the Word, one with the Father and the Holy Spirit, His 'place', the nature of the humanity which the Word assumed, the 'place' of this humanity, and the relation between the two 'places'.

The dispute was between the Lutherans and the Calvinists. But before that dispute can be analysed, it is necessary to look at the origin and nature of the bases which determined the theological outlook of the Lutherans.

Luther carried into his later theological thought a great deal of his legacy in past training. Generally this means certain emphases and traits of mind engendered by the ethos of mediaeval scholasticism. It is clear from the terminology which he employs that part of that inheritance which he still used owes much to Aristotelian influence. It is a mistake, it may be noted, to dismiss all mediaeval thought as being under the yoke of Aristotle. Duns Scotus and Robert Grosseteste in particular were critics – and at times severe critics – of Aristotelian philosophy.

They were by no means alone. The marginal notes in MS. F96 – Averroës' (Ibn Rushd): *Commentary on Aristotle's Physica*, in Worcester Cathedral Library – generally agreed to be notes taken during Oxford lectures, betray a high criticism of Aristotelianism. The later John Major, after his work in Paris, Rector of St Andrew's University, likewise was a severe critic of that tendency in the prevailing theological emphasis of the late Middle Ages. This anti-Aristotelian emphasis was not a concentratedly insular English and Scottish phenomenon. For it was not without its counterpart on the Continent, as may be instanced from time to time in the Paris theologians.

Major himself had influence upon the studies undertaken in Paris, while the earlier Robert Curzon (de Courcon) who was regent there from 1204–1210/11, acting as Papal Legate, banned the Aristotelian physical writings in 1210. Grosseteste seems to have been well known to important figures in the French Church, according to Matthew Paris[16], among them, Curzon, Abbot Eustace of Flay, a noted Cistercian, Master Jacobus de Vitry, and Stephen Langton on his French sojourn.

There was much coming and going between England and Paris in any case. It was the traditional place for English clerks to further their theological education. Edmund of Abingdon was one such illustrious scholar, and, as James McEvoy points out[17] Bulaeus asserts[18] that Grosseteste himself studied there for a time – which explains Grosseteste's familiarity with the nature of theological studies in France.

Although Grosseteste took the Arabic commentaries, and used them in his own works – often in his interpretation as a means of criticising Aristotle – the Aristotelian emphases of these commentaries became acceptable and regarded as fundamental, without criticism of the main tenets of that philosophical system, in Paris after 1220. Aristotelianism, after the stricture imposed in the early 13th century, became the philosophical and theological norm from the second quarter of the 13th century onwards. The reason for this was the influence of Aquinas who persuasively and ably was the advocate for the philosophical norms of Aristotelianism.

Though these principles of philosophical approach were treated and re-interpreted in a more dynamic way than previously, and thus re-presented in a modified form by Thomist thought, yet nevertheless the spectre of Aristotle, partly exorcised by that critical approach of thinking in accordance with the nature of objective realities – an approach represented by Grosseteste and later continued by Duns Scotus – reappeared to haunt and entice theological activity and endeavour.

The monumental brilliance and persuasiveness of Aquinas assured the foreseeable future for an Aristotelian emphasis in theological endeavour. In any case, both Grosseteste and Duns Scotus were tainted to a degree with suspicion and uncertainty, the first because of his stalwart and robust criticism not of the office of the Papacy itself but of the way Papal authority was construed and exercised, and because of his patronage of the Franciscans, the other because he was a Franciscan.

It should not be without comment that neither Grosseteste nor Duns Scotus were canonized, yet Aquinas was so exalted forty-nine years after his death.

The spread of his influence was no doubt assisted through the regard in which the comparitively new Dominican order, of which he became a member after his initial alliance with the Benedictines, was held and through the influence it had with the Papacy.

The reading and study of Aquinas's work was forbidden by the Franciscans for some time, and Aquinas was not without his critics closer at home, as instanced by the reservations and criticisms of some of his propositions by Archbishop Kilwardy (d.1279), himself a Dominican and not without Aristotelian leanings. Such criticism and opposition continued as may be seen from the attitude of the much later John Major in Paris. Thomist thought still had its constant, if isolated, critics – those tending towards objective reasoning and κατὰ φύσιν (according to the nature of objective realities) thinking up to the beginning of the 16th century and the eve of the Reformation.

But it was this generally accepted philosophical emphasis of Aristotelian influence in theology throughout Europe which was the training ground for Luther. Just how much dependency there was on this Aristotelian legacy is clear in the Lutheran stand in the dispute with the Calvinists.

With regard to *space*, Aristotle radically misinterpreted Plato. It is this particular mistaken construing of Platonic thought and in the subsequent Lutheran acceptance of

the Aristotelian deviance, that the core of this dispute is
found.

Plato developed that notion of space which stretched back
through the history of Greek thought to the inception of the
philosophy of the Pythagoreans and the Atomists. Such a
view regarded space as a *container* or a *receptacle*. This, in
various forms, pervaded the long sweep of Greek thinking in
general.

Plato's development, however, was to treat this description
of space metaphorically, for he eschewed that terminology
which implies that space can be described in terms of volume
or quantity.

Space, in Platonic thought, is to be distinguished from the
objects within it. It provides the situation (a word which
implies place and therefore tangibility and measurability, but
in Plato's usage is shorn of all such connotations) for the
existence of all that comes into being. It is a medium
($\dot{\epsilon}\kappa\mu\alpha\gamma\epsilon\hat{\iota}o\nu$) which, being both without form and passive, is
not a confining and determining receptacle of the things
which it contains. The emphasis is on the provision made by
space for events which occur and whereby, in the universal
rationality of these events as things come into being, change
and move, the nature of space may be hesitatingly and
partially perceived, rather than the relation of space to the
actual objects as measurable entities within it. In other
words we have here what is in essence a dynamic approach
to the question of the nature of space rather than a static
perception of it.

This approach is heightened by Plato's seeming attempt to
regard space as that which is necessary in the attempt to
overcome the chasm ($\chi\omega\rho\iota\sigma\mu\acute{o}s$) – the separation – between
the realm of the intelligible and the world of the sensible,
between the 'ideal' and the 'real', the 'spiritual' and the
'tangible', the realm of the 'archetypes' ($\pi\alpha\rho\alpha\delta\epsilon\acute{\iota}\gamma\mu\alpha\tau\alpha$) and
that of the 'copies' ($\mu\iota\mu\acute{\eta}\mu\alpha\tau\alpha$). The things which come into
being, exist and move and change in this world, the sensible,
are copies of the archetypes in the realm of the heavenly or
the ideal, the intelligible.

Space, in Plato's view, is a third category between the
archetypes and the copies. For, while it does not contain the

archetypes, the copies 'in' space are only copies because of it. If it were not for space, then the events which occur within it as the medium which permits all this, would not have their specific nature and configuration as copies. Space, therefore, is the means by which they are permitted both to be themselves and also, as that, to be copies of the archetypes. Space thus bridges the gap between the intelligible and the sensible.

A significant misinterpretation of Plato's view of space by Aristotle is that he viewed Plato as believing the distinction between the archetypes and the copies, the χορισμὸς, the gulf, between the two worlds of the intelligible and the sensible, to be a spatial one. Space for him was in the same category as the objects within it and was a volumetric matter.

In following this view, Aristotle perceived space as the prime stuff from which all things derived and took their nature. Space, in such an interpretation, becomes that which is looked upon as a closed container of all things. It thereby exercises a causal force upon them. The Aristotelian view of space was that its primacy did not elevate it in quality more than other things, but did so in quantity – there is only magnitude, but even such a magnitude is finite.

Here his observations on *place* have to be introduced in order to elucidate further his concept of space. Space is a *continuous quantity* filled with matter and which embraces objects which have a common boundary with the space they occupy. The particular part of space occupied by an object or body is its *place*. This definition of place is reinforced by his observations that when an object moves, or is replaced by another sort of object, we are to think of place as something different from these various and varying place-occupying objects. His illustration[19] is that the independence of place is obvious in that when water has gone out as from a vessel it is replaced by air – so another body occupies that space which is different from both the first occupant and the second. Its difference lies in the distinction between the container and the contained.

There is also a distinction between *place* as that which is the place of bodies, which place they have in common – κοινὸς τόπος – *common place*, and *exact* or *proper place* – ἴδιος τόπος – which is the place occupied by a particular body and no other[20]. *Place*, therefore is that which is the immediate compass of each body or bodies, its limit being co-terminous and simultaneous to the outer limit of the occupying body[21].

It would seem that this distinction leads to the idea that space is extended place (the *common place* of all bodies and objects), and is yet divisible into exact parts or apportionments (the *proper place* of a particular body or object). So, in its totality as an extendible finitude, space is the total container of all things, and, as such, is the greatest and prime thing.

How far this view has permeated into a common, though unconscious, way of thinking about things is evidenced by the universal phrases *in space, in place*. Something is construed and described as being *in place*.

It is this background but controlling view of space which coloured the Lutheran interpretation of the incarnation. The humanity of Christ was, for Lutheran theology, the place of the eternal Word in redemptive and revealing act. As such, the humanity is the container of the Word. It must be said in fairness to Lutheran theological aims that the concern was for the real and actual union of the divine and human natures as the one Person, Jesus Christ. Any suggestion that the two natures were separate, or even loosely conjoined, was abhorrent. But such was the mediaeval background of Lutheranism, with the prevailing Aristotelian interpretations of space and place, that the union of the divinity to the humanity was put forth in terms of the divine Word being poured into the container of the humanity.

Calvinism clearly saw that there were several related issues raised by this.

The first was that there was a tendency to a confusion of the natures, since the limits of the humanity and the limits of the divine Word therein contained were co-terminous.

The second was the question of the nature of the Word. A claim such as that which Lutheranism proposed meant that the Word was Himself capable of limitation in such a way that his essential nature as the One by whom all things were made, sustained and upheld, was compromised. The Calvinist question 'Who ruled the universe if the Word was so contained completely within the limits of the human nature?' was apposite.

On the other hand, the Lutherans countered this by posing what they saw as a problem raised by the Calvinist objection, that if the Word was not so totally united to the humanity, then the incarnation was a Nestorian matter of a separation and a loose conjunction of the natures.

The issue developed with the Calvinist reply that 'While He (the Divine Word in union with the humanity) lay cradled on his mother's knee, he yet ruled the heavens'. The 'place' of the Word was both in lowliness in Bethlehem, the 'place' of humanity, the space of the created dimension, and yet on the heavenly throne of cosmic rule and majesty, one with the Father and the Spirit, the 'place' of God, the 'space' of Deity.

In all this the Calvinists were being faithful to the patristic commentaries on this question. Athanasius had written quite clearly on the matter of the Word's existence and the humanity he assumed[22]:

> For He was not, as might be imagined, circumscribed in the body, nor, while present in the body, was He absent elsewhere; nor, while He moved in the body, was the universe left void of His working and Providence; but, thing most marvellous, Word as He was, so far from being contained by anything, He rather contained all things Himself ... thus, even while present in a human body and Himself quickening it, He was, without inconsistency, quickening the universe as well, and was in every process of nature, and was outside the whole, and while known from the body by His works, He was none the less manifest from the working of the universe as well ... for He was not bound to His body, but rather was Himself wielding it, so that He was not only in it, but was actually in everything, and while external to the universe, abode in His Father only ... So that not even when the Virgin bore Him did He suffer any change, nor by being in the body was [His glory] dulled ...

Gregory of Nyssa wrote in like vein[23], and, in so doing, made it abundantly clear that while we may acknowledge that the Word became incarnate, we cannot ask 'how?' this came about, anymore than we can ask 'how?' creation was brought into existence. Gregory of Nyssa links the miracle – for that is the theological word used – of the incarnation, with regard to it being God's act and therefore indefinable, with the miracle of creation as being likewise the act of God incapable of human analysis and explanation.

'But the nature of man', it is said, 'is narrow and circumscribed, whereas the Deity is infinite. How could the Deity be included in the atom?' But who is it that says the infinitude of the Deity is comprehended in the envelopment of the flesh as if it were in a vessel? ... What is there, then, to prevent our ... guarding the proper notion of Deity, believing as we do that, though the Godhead be in man, it is beyond all circumscription ... God was born in the nature of man. But how – this, as being a subject unapproachable by the processes of reasoning, we decline to investigate. For though we believe, as we do, that all the corporeal and intellectual creation derives its subsistence from the incorporeal and uncreated Being, yet the WHENCE or the HOW, these we do not make a matter for examination along with our faith in the thing itself. While we accept the fact, we pass by the manner of the putting together of the Universe, as a subject which must not be curiously handled, but one altogether ineffable and inexplicable.

It is noteworthy that here Gregory of Nyssa assumes the fact that the world of ideas – the intellectual creation – has, like the sensible world, the material creation, a beginning. There is no Platonism here. All that is apart from God is created. What is underlying here is the tacit awareness that such is the Infinity which God is, His Infinity cannot be examined in terms of, or compared with, any created dimension – not even that which we call 'infinite'. The 'infinities' of space are not to be construed in the same way as the Infinity of God. For even if these infinities are beyond human comprehension, they nevertheless are pertaining to creation and not to God.

John of Damascus (c.675–c.749) later, too, had a quite clear idea of what was at stake in the incarnation of the Word. He states it succinctly[24]:

Without separating from the Father's bosom, the Word dwelt in the bosom of the holy virgin ... thus in all and over all He was Himself, when He existed in the bosom of the holy bearer of God.

We have to recognize that we must distinguish between

infinities to do with the created order – infinities of whatever dimension – and the uncreated Infinity which God is in his Being. It is this distinction which is thrown into sharp focus by the consideration of the incarnation. For what was at stake in the Lutheran/Calvinist dispute was the idea of quantity, or mathematical infinity in relation to the finite. The warfare was engaged on the Lutheran side on the question of the relation of concepts of infinity to the finite; on the Calvinist and patristic side, the relation of the indescribable and ineffable Infinite to that whole dimension which is characterised by finitude and conceptual ideas of infinity gleaned from temporal and spatial considerations.

In all this, the Calvinists were adhering to the patristic view of the incarnation of the Word as expressed by the Nicene fathers. The Lutherans, on the other hand, were still operating with an Aristotelian type view of space as a container, and things in space as containers, and with the inability or unwillingness to depart from a mathematical/philosophical concept of infinity. Hence the humanity of Christ is regarded by them as the container of the Word, and the Word thereby circumscribed – which is a comment on the fact that conceptual ideas of infinity are ultimately contained by finitude. The quantitive nature of their concept of infinity, and applying that infinity to the Word, is highlighted by the jibe with which they described the Calvinist position – the 'Extra Calvinisticum'. That is, they thought that the Calvinists were of the same mind as they with regard to the nature of infinity, and this meant that the Calvinists were saying that some quantity of the Word was 'extra', 'outside' the humanity of Christ.

What we may and only properly call the Infinite and what we perceive to be the 'finite' (which must now include spatial and temporal 'infinities') are centred on the Word made flesh and anchored in the divine life of the Trinity. The issue is one of existence – the life of the created dimension on the one hand, and the being of God on the other, and their binding together without compromising their identities in the Word made flesh.

The distinction between such 'infinity' and the Infinity which God is, had not gone unrecognized in previous gener-

ations of theologians. It is to one of these that we will be
turning later, his contribution – sadly neglected – to this
question. This was Robert Grosseteste (c.1170–1253) with
his assertion that all our infinities are finite to God, and the
subsequent understanding of space which opened out from
this. We now turn to examine the question of the double
contingency of creation – its distinction from, and its dependence upon, God, and the relation of the incarnation to
creation for an understanding, as following from what has
been set out in this chapter, of space in its relation to God.

6

Recapitulation, Contingency and Space

THE INCARNATION stands central to the Doctrine of Recapitulation – the summing up of all things into a head. Indeed, recapitulation is but a statement of the significance of the incarnation and what is achieved and accomplished by the Word made flesh.

This doctrine's biblical foundation is found particularly and explicitly in the *Epistle to the Colossians* and the *Epistle to the Ephesians*. It lies implicitly elsewhere, for example in the prologue to *St John's Gospel*, the *Epistle to the Romans*, the *Epistle to the Philippians*, the *Epistle to the Hebrews* and in the *Apocalypse*. Nor is without its Old Testament antecedents, for example, again, in Isaiah's references to God's action in bringing about the new heavens and the new earth.

One of the key concepts found in those patristic works which deal with recapitulation is that *the end* is joined to *the beginning*. Tertullian states this clearly[1]:

> So too, the two letters of Greece, the first and the last, the Lord assumes to Himself, as figures of the beginning and end which concur in Himself; so that, just as Alpha rolls on till it reaches Omega, and again Omega rolls back until it reaches Alpha, in the same way He might show that in Himself is both the downward course of the beginning on to the end, and the backward course of the end up to the beginning; so that every economy [that is, ordering], ending in Him through whom it began – through the Word of God, that is, Who was made flesh – may have an end corresponding to its beginning. And so truly in Christ are all things recalled to the beginning.

This is parallel to what Pascal was to say much later[2] concerning the created reality as

> an infinite sphere whose centre is everywhere and circumference nowhere

97

these extremities of centre and circumference meeting and conjoining in God. At least, we may see a parallel provided we interpret Pascal's 'infinities' to be such only to our limited minds but finite to God who is alone the Infinite.

What, of course, Pascal did not say, as Tertullian states, was that such a meeting and conjoining are a Christological event. Both, however, from their sundry times and diverse positions, were talking about the whole of the created reality, the totality of existence. It is this totality which concerns us in the Doctrine of Recapitulation. This totality is biblically expressed.

> All things were made by him; and without him was not anything made that was made.[3]
> That in the dispensation of the fulness of times he might gather together in one all things in Christ, both which are in heaven, and which are on earth; even in him.[4]
> For by him were all things created, that are in heaven, and that are in earth, visible and invisible, whether they be thrones, or dominions, or principalities, or powers; all things were created by him, and for him:
> And he is before all things, and in him all things consist ... For it pleased the Father that in him should all fulness dwell.[5]

The absolute inclusiveness of the word *all* should not be doubted. This is the declaration that the totality of all that is, that exists in its otherness to God, is related to the One by whom all things were made, in its creation and in its fulfilment, in its beginning and in its end.

But, according to Irenaeus in his remarkable development of the Doctrine of Recapitulation, both in his *Adversus Haereses* and his *Demonstration of the Apostolic Preaching*, what is also not to be doubted here is that these are declarations of a relation between Creator and creature which is not static or even mechanical. They are concerned with being and action – the Being and action of the Creator primarily and explicitly, and the being and movement of the creation towards its fulfilment secondarily and implicitly. Moreover, the inner and full meaning of all creation is found in this relation. For this relation is characterized by the creation, dispensation and gathering of this all by God. It is within this that all things live, move and have their being.

This involves us in two considerations: 1. That the universe can only be understood in its open-ness to God in whom it finds its raison-d'etre and its ultimate meaning – *all things were created for him and by him.* 2. That humanity occupies a central and indispensable role in the inter-relations of God and this universe – *the Word became flesh and dwelt among us: that ... he might gather together in one all things.*

1. The most recent scientific views of the cosmos are that it is to be understood as a whole, in which each constituent element, whether microscopic or macroscopic, interacts in a profoundly related way to all the rest. Moreover, no longer is there the closed mechanical attitude to the cosmos which thinks that it is self-explanatory and self-sufficient and can be understood out of itself.

This is far from that mechanistic world-view which developed from Newton's petrified system of interpreting all things in terms of absolute time and absolute space, wherein the universe was regarded both, as explainable by mechanical formulae and mathematical computation, and also, as composed of separated elements and entities which, though they interacted one with another through empty space, could be isolated and examined in isolation.

The former had the effect of advocating a closed universe in which everything was to be interpreted by a system of cause and effect which leads to a deterministic view of all things; the latter the effect of a disregard of the fact that things are to be understood not just out of themselves but also in their relations with other things – an attitude which can lead to a malevolent technology since it ignored the inter-relational aspects of the essential nature of entities.

In other words, in all this view, physical theory and law is made to exist in isolation from the ontological realities as they exist in themselves as entities inter-related to, and interacting with, other fields and levels of existences. Order is construed as mechanical, compartmentalized and deterministic.

This is far from the concept of 'order' as perceived by, for example, Irenaeus, Athanasius and Basil, which permeated the thought of the early Church, or from the concept of order which prevails in scientific attitudes after such great strides have been made both in the astrophysical fields of the universe and in the microscopic aspects of existence. Relativity theory as it has developed and is developing, as with quantum theory and mechanics, exhibit a vastly different posture as to how we should regard the universe and the whole question of existence.

It was all too easy with the former view, both to equate the absolute framework of the universe with an immutable, unmoving God – the shadow of Aristotle – and in its deterministic, inbuilt and introverted necessities stemming from that framework, to disregard and discard any idea of freedom and contingency. It was, in essence, a fatalistic synthesis of ultimate, theoretically infinite causes and fixed, immanent laws.

But the later developments, in some respects found in Faraday's scientific contribution, certainly in Clerk Maxwell's achievements, and on through Einstein's revolution and all that the post-Einsteinian scientific community is achieving, bear many parallels of thought to the way that theology, as emphasised by Irenaeus and the Nicene fathers, has struggled to interpret creation.

Science, of course, begins with the created verities and works upwards, as it were, to the boundaries of creation; theology begins with the Self-revelation of the Triune God as Father, Son and Holy Spirit, the sufficient and free Creator, and in that light looks at creation. There is every possibility of inter-action and mutual benefit of knowledge – if theology stands as theology and science as science, not confused and falsely mixing, but holding to their respective integrities, in which they converse with and question each other, and both not the bondservants of extraneous conceptual attitudes and pressures which are the relics and echoes of the outmoded and damaging mechanical-rationalist era of thought and practice regarding creation and existence which still occupy general thought, more instructive attitudes not yet having permeated into the popular mind and replaced the commonly accepted.

From theology's side, the universe is to be regarded as that which is created by God to be in relation, in its totality and, within that totality, in its diversity, to him, and therefore open to him. From that of science, the awe and respect for the created realities revealing themselves in their immensities and intensities in all the rational order in the midst and indeed out of the apparently chaotic complexities, fields of related existences opening out to that which lies beyond them and gives them ultimate meaning.

2. This unity of creation and this relation with the Creator stems from the consideration of the incarnation of the Word by whom all things were made. Central to this is the place of humanity in creation. The theologians of the fourth century, and before them Irenaeus in the second, did not treat humanity as being in sole creative relation with God to the exclusion of all else.

To remove humanity from the created sphere with all its levels of existence, would be to remove humanity from its 'place' in space, and make it an abstraction. There is no such abstract theory of humanity found in their works. Rather, humanity is regarded as firmly anchored within this context of all creation and with an indispensable estate and office in relation to that in which it lives, moves and has its being.

This centrality of humanity is a matter of dispute in the scientific community, which regards this as the *anthropic principle* either to be accepted or rejected. Most of those who reject it also reject the theological claim that creation has a purpose, that is, the rejection of the *anthropic principle* goes hand in hand with the rejection of the *teleological principle*, though in some cases, for example in the work of Brandon Carter[6], an anthropic principle is accepted in the weak form that the fact humanity exists may determine some of the characteristics of the universe which we observe, but has no bearing on a possible purpose for the universe.

One cannot help but ask that if there is no purpose in the universe then what is the purpose of any human achievement whatsoever? Why bother? save for mere convenience, and so much of even that is a struggle to gain. Indeed, the further question could be put, 'Why write books pointing out that there is no purpose if there be no purpose?'!

Whatever the outcome, if any, in the scientific debate, the centrality and significance of humanity in creation has been a theological principle. While some early theologians dwelt on it and gave it absolute importance more than others did, it was generally accepted throughout the Christian thought of the first four centuries. In any case, the idea of the determinative significance of the centrality of humanity for all creation, and as characterising the whole creative purpose of God, has a long hinterland in the Old Testament which is deemed to find its fulfilment in the New Testament.

In the narrative of Genesis, the creation of Adam is highlighted by the employment of the Hebrew verb for 'let us make' – in place of 'let there be' which prefaces every other creative act of God. Lancelot Andrewes elaborated on this[7]:

> To shew this, we divide His workes, (as we have warrant) into His workes of Fiat (as the rest of His creatures:) and the Worke of Faciamus, as Man, the master-peece of His workes; upon whom He did more cost, shewed more workemanship, than on the rest: the very word [Faciamus] sets him above all.1. ... that Hee did deliberate, enter into consultation (as it were) about his making, and about none else. 2. ... that Himselfe framed his body of the mould, as the potter, the clay. 3. ... Then, that He breathed into him a two-lived soule, which made the Psalmist breake out, Domine, quid est homo &c? Lord, what is man, thou shouldest so regard him, as to passe by the heavens and all the glorious bodies there, and passing by them, breathe an immortal soule, put thine own image, upon a peece of clay? 4. But last, God's setting him Super *omnia opera manuum suarum*, over all the workes of His hands. Making him (as I may say) Counte palatine of the worlde; this shewes plainely, His setting by man more than all of them. As he, then, over them; so, God's mercy over him. Over all His workes, over this worke. Over His chiefe worke, chiefly: in a higher degree.

Andrewes goes on to elaborate further on the need of man for God's mercy, as he of all creatures is liable to fall, and has fallen, from God. What is noteworthy is that he goes on to link creation and incarnation. God's mercy is expressed in the fact that

> another workemanship He hath yet; His workemanship in Christ Jesus; the Apostle calls it (Ephes 2.10) His new creature (Gal. 6.15) ... the Saviour of all men ... They are His worke wrought on both sides; Creation on one side, Redemption on the other.

Andrewes regards creation and incarnation as the one act of God – one work with two sides. Moreover, the context of this passage makes it clear that there is no disjunction between God's act and God's being. His being is expressed in His acts and His acts are an expression of His being. Creation and re-creation, as the one act of God, are accomplished in relation to His being. Central to and *chiefest* of this work is the existence of humanity – but humanity only in the context of Christ, in whom humanity is united, in the human nature of Christ, to the divine life of the Triune God.

The centrality of man in creation is understood theologically in the light of Christology. It is not a question of seeing the centrality of humanity on the basis of humanity considered in relation to other created orders, and interpreted within that created dimension alone. Rather, it is the assertion that humanity occupies a central and significant role in creation because of its special relation to the Creator. For the existence of humanity is directly related, without compromising its created nature, to the existence of God, without compromising the divine nature.

The role of humanity in creation is further seen in that relation, in that its knowledge of creation can only be properly gained in the light of its knowledge of God. Indeed, as John Calvin pointed out at the very beginning of his *Institute of the Christian Religion*[8]

> ... it is evident that man never attains to a true self-knowledge until he have previously contemplated the face of God, and come down after such contemplation to look at himself.

The basic rule behind such an attitude is *in thy light we see light*[9]. It also follows that this attitude, as in this quotation from the Psalms, couples light, which is knowledge and understanding, and life together. Indeed, creation is regarded as bounded by the first act of creation, the bringing of created light, analogous in its dimension to God's uncreated light, and the last act of creation, the making of man. In other words creation is characterized from first to last and in its continuance, by rationality – light giving both illumination and mental enlightenment and man being a rational creature receptive of both functions of light. Moreover, both light and humanity are in relation to the Creator, the one reflecting Uncreated light, the rationality and order which God is in Himself, and the other likewise being made in the image of God, reflecting, in the composition and nature of humanity as inter-personal, the inter-Personal relation within the Trinity.

Light and human being coalesce, as it were, in the Word made flesh. As Light of light He is also man. Moreover, the light-founded and therefore rational existence of humanity in its relation to its Creator is emphasised by the Word as the personalising Person, by whom all is created, Himself Light and Life, and the human as a personalised person.

The seventeenth century theologian, John Swan, also emphasises the particular significance, estate and office of humanity in his *Speculum Mundi*, which also contains his *Hexameron*[10].

> Though mankind were the last, yet not the least. God onely spake his powerfull word, and then the other creatures were produced: but now he calls a counsel, and doth consult, not out of need, but rather to shew the excellencie of his work; or indeed, to shew himself: He speaks not therefore to the Angels but the Trinitie, saying, Let us make man. Wherein the Father, as the first in order, speaketh to the Sonne and holy Spirit; and the Sonne and Spirit, speak and decree it with the Father: and the Father, Sonne and Holy Ghost, all Three in One, and One in Three, create a creature to be the other creatures lord. He was therefore the last, as the end of all the rest; the last in execution, but first in intention; the Map, Epitome, and Compendium of all the rest.

Here we have a concept of order and man's estate and vocation in the minds of the time. This especial work of God is seen as a matter in which the Divine rationality is exercised in the counsel taken, the decree made, by the Persons of the Trinity in their unity and distinction. What rationality man has as a creature is therefore in immediate correspondence to that uncreated rationality which is God's. As with created light (upon which Swan elaborates in his commentary in the *Hexameron* on the first day's work) with uncreated light, so here with created rational existence and the uncreated Rationality which is God.

But man is also related to all other things within the created dimension. He is both the reason for their existence and, in his existence, the sum or *compendium* of them all. As their *epitome*, His existence sums up theirs. As their *map*, the knowledge of them is centred on, and springs from, him. This privileged position of humanity is elaborated upon by Swan[11]:

> God made the world for Man, and Man for himself. It was therefore a daintie fancie of one, who brought in the World speaking to Man after this manner ... '*Vide homo, dicit Mundus* ... See oh man, (saith the World) how he hath loved thee, who made me for thee. I serve thee, because I am made for thee, that thou maist serve him who made both me and thee; me for thee, and thee for himself.'

So humanity stands, as it were, on the borders between the temporal and spatial entities and their Creator. As set out in the thought of these 17th century instances, humanity also bears relation to the totality of creation. It is for this reason that so many of the 17th century writers on the subject of the creation of man, can regard man as a *microcosm*. In the sense of the relativities and relations of the created orders in their totality, humanity sums them up.

In all this the 17th century writers mentioned above are merely interpreting in their own fashion observations on the creation on man from the early church. A reading of Gregory of Nyssa's *On the Making of Man*, his contribution to the unfinished *Hexaemeron* of St Basil, particularly sections II –X, together with a reading of the relevant sections of Swan's *Hexameron*, or Purchas's *His Pilgrimage*, show the indebtedness of these later writers to such patristic commentaries.

It is the earlier Irenaeus (c.AD 122–202), however, who first sets out systematically the relation of man to all the orders of creation in his doctrine of recapitulation. This is found in both his *Adversus Haereses* and in the shorter work, which seems to be written as an *enchiridion* of the Christian faith, summarising the positive sections, and missing out the condemnatory sections on the gnostic heresies, of the larger and earlier work[12].

Irenaeus, in the *Demonstration of the Apostolic Preaching*, first sets out the nature of the Christian faith.

Here there is a strong, objective, κατὰ φύσιν, emphasis on the acquirement of knowledge[13].

> Faith rests on things that truly are. For in things that are, as they are, we truly believe; and believing in things that are, as they ever are, we keep firm our confidence in them.

The Christian faith is not only a matter of the intellect, but also of the quality of life. Among all other theological considerations which are implied in this, the important one for our purposes here is that it demonstrates that for Irenaeus there was no disjunction between the world of the intelligible and the world of the sensible, no gulf between mind and being, and therefore no lurking dualism of form and content, idea and fact. We think of things as they truly are in themselves. And as we think, so we act. The theological mind must have a corresponding deportment of being and acting. Thus[14]:

> For godliness is obscured and dulled by the soiling and the staining of the flesh, and is broken and polluted and no more entire, if falsehood enter into the soul: but it will keep itself in its beauty and measure, when truth is constant in the soul and purity in the flesh. For what profit is it to know the truth in words, and to pollute the flesh and perform the works of evil? Or what profit can purity of flesh bring, if truth be not in the soul? For these rejoice with one another, and are united and allied to bring man face to face with God.

The estate and vocation of humanity is indispensably bound with the requirement to know God and to know the creation in which God has set human being. Man's existence and raison d'être is a life and calling fundamentally of rationality. And rationality, theologically, means both mental perception and corresponding quality of existence and activity. The existence of humanity as part of the temporal/spatial dimension will exhibit a rational appreciation of the nature of that created sphere – and this means the acknowledgement of its contingency to God, its dependence upon him for its beginning and upholding and purpose, and its contingency from God, its created nature, identity and freedom as an entity other than God.

The freedom of creation to be creation, what it really is in itself, is not however to be perceived as a freedom from God, but a freedom for God or towards God, for only in this sort of freedom can it maintain its integrity. It is humanity's status and role to set out and interpret this double contingency, and, on the basis of such thoughts to exist and act accordingly.

It is in the context of this double contingency that the doctrine of recapitulation is developed. But this double contingency is expressed first and foremost, and in a unique way, in the incarnation, where, as Irenaeus says[15], we perceive

> The Word ... revealing God indeed to men, but presenting man to God.

Athanasius later took this up (as he did with so many of the themes of Irenaeus) and echoes the earlier church Father by saying[16]:

> ... our Lord, being Word and Son of God, bore a body, and became Son of Man, that, having become Mediator between God and men, He might minister the things of God to us and things of ours to God.

We have here the existence of God being brought to bear on the created realities at the centre of which stands humanity. The double contingency is expressed in this unique way here, in that, the Word of God, one with the Father and the Spirit, yet himself the Word other than the Father and the Spirit, takes our human existence to himself, and is born the child Jesus in Bethlehem of Judaea. This he does without compromising, diluting, changing or forsaking his 'Godness'. He, by whom all things are created and for whom they are created and in whom they consist, takes human flesh and nature to himself and makes it his own. The Creator, in other words, becomes one of his own creatures, but remains the Creator.

We seek to understand and describe this, without trespassing on the 'how' of God and explaining his mode of being and operation away, by way of the employment of two Greek terms – ἀνυπόστασις and ἐνυπόστασις, anhupostasis and enhupostasis.

The first when applied to the question of the two natures of Christ, the divine and the human, states that without union with the existence of the Word, the humanity of Christ would have no existence at all. The second states that within that union with the existence of the Word, the humanity does have existence as humanity. There is no man Jesus who exists apart from the fact that he is the Word of God incarnate. His identity and individuality is created and established by and in – and only by and in – this union.

In a unique way, for no other created reality is in relation to God in this personal way, we have here a statement of double contingency; the humanity is utterly dependent for its being and identity on the Divine Word – the contingency of the human nature of Christ TO the Word – yet it has its own identity and nature as humanity in that union – the contingency of the human nature FROM the Word.

However, contingency in general is not as this, for only the humanity of Christ is in union with the Word. All other things exist in their contingent relation to God by the grace and loving kindness of the Word. Nor, as at the ascension of our Lord whereby the humanity is taken into the internal life of the Triune God, does anything else so exist as the existence of God. All other things exist in relation to, but not as, the existence of God.

We may perhaps say that the double contingency of creation is itself contingent on this unique double contingency of the human nature of Christ to and from the divine nature.

In *The Anachronism of Time*, I have argued that all time, time in its totality from its beginning to its end, exists as a dynamic present in its relation to God [17]. God is not bound by the passing of time which we call 'past, present and future', as though some endless line of time were the dimension which God inhabited. Gregory of Nyssa's observation on the existence of God [18] is pertinent:

> ... the existence which is all-sufficient, everlasting, world-enveloping, is not in space, nor in time: it is before these, and above these in an ineffable way; self-contained, knowable by faith alone; immeasurable by ages; without the accompaniment of time; seated and resting in itself, with no association of past or future, there being nothing beside and beyond itself, whose passing can make something past and something future. Such accidents are confined to the creation, whose life is divided with time's divisions into memory and hope. But within that transcendent and blessed Power all things are

equally present as in an instant: past and future are within its all-encircling grasp and its comprehensive view.

Or again[19]:

The Divine nature is a stranger to these special marks of creation: It leaves beneath itself the sections of time, the 'before' and the 'after', and the ideas of space: in fact 'higher' cannot properly be said of it at all.

The 'moment' of creation and the 'moment' of incarnation are therefore, on this basis, to be regarded as 'instantaneous' to God. Indeed, it would be folly for our doctrine of God to regard the incarnation as some sort of divine afterthought – that God, having set creation in being, realised that he had made something which had become out of control and decided to intervene. This view projects time concepts into God and makes God subservient to, or contingent upon, time and its movement.

It seems to me that behind a great deal of patristic and mediaeval thought, there is a lingering attempt to point to this idea of all time, and therefore all things and all space, being a dynamic present to God. That is to say, that while we think in terms of what we call the past, which for us is no more, and the future, which has no substance for it is not yet, and the present, which cannot be measured so infinitesimal it is – all of which is but a convenience of category and measurement – all this is to God present in all its reality in a way that we cannot comprehend..

I posit the idea that what for us is the past, the future and the present are held 'instantly' (though this word itself has temporal connotations) in a present which, unlike our present is fulfilled dynamically as the totality of our past and future.

In support of this argument I used the illustration of the single beam of light which is refracted into its constituent colours. The refraction with its spectrum of the various colours is this dimension in which we live, move along and through that spectrum as through the aeons, the centuries, the years, the months, the weeks, the days, the moments, and have our temporal and spatial being. To us it appears as a straight line, and we measure time accordingly. But to God it is as the single beam, which recapitulates all the constituent parts in a singularity.

This too, I would seek to interpret Christologically. The juxtaposition of creation and incarnation, I have also argued in *The Anachronism of Time*, whereby they are two sides of the one act of God, means that incarnation is not something which happens merely at a given point[20]. Of course it does – from our side of experiencing the refracted one act of God into its spatial and temporal dimensions. But it is more than that. I would suggest that it is the way in which God creates, recognizing that to create an entity other than himself is to create an reality which is vulnerable and requires constant upholding and re-creation in its refracted dimension, and involving his Being in that creation and upholding. The incarnation is the taking of the created realities to himself and bearing their frailty, so preserving their integrity and their identity. The incarnation is the cost to God of creating.

The *Let there be ... Let us make ...* is accomplished in terms of *the Word was made flesh*. Hence, the patristic interpretation of Proverbs VIII:22ff (in the Septuagint version) – *the Lord created me a beginning (ἀρχή) of His ways for His works* – in which the *me* refers to the Wisdom of God identified by the early Church with Christ, takes on a more profound meaning, and one towards which, perhaps, the patristic writers were feeling, namely that the incarnation is the principle of creation, the beginning in which the beginning of all things is found. This opens out all that Athanasius interprets in calling Christ the Ἀρχή Ὁδῶν, the *Arche Hodon*, the *Beginning of ways* in his works against the Arians[21], or his reference to him as Ὁ Κυριακὸς Ἀνθρωπος, *Ho Kuriakos Anthropos*, the *Dominical Man.*[22]

The Word made flesh is The Image of God (for he is what he images) while humanity, the characteristic of all creation, is made *in the image of God and after His likeness*. The Word and the flesh which he takes in union with himself, and is thereby Dominical Man, the Beginning of Ways, images the relation of the Father and the Word bound in the bond of divine love, the Holy Spirit, a relational existence of unity in diversity, while the composition of humanity, as an inter-personal existence images this in its solely spatial/temporal dimension.

Irenaeus describes Adam, whom he regards as the recapitulation of all humanity, as *the ancient formation, the protoplasm, the archetype*[23]. But he equally regards Christ as recapitulating, that is, gathering up, Adam, in the Word's taking human flesh and nature into union with Himself. It is Adamic flesh which the Word assumes, that is, humanity under the judgment of God, for Adam is regarded as the recapitulative history of all humanity. When Adam falls, all fall – or, if it is preferred, the plight of humanity is summed up in the story of Adam. But if the incarnation is the principle of creation, is it not that the description of Adam *as the ancient formation, the protoplasm, the archetype*, refers in the first instance to the humanity of the Word? Gregory of Nyssa explicitly calls Christ the *Prototype*[24] of humanity. I would regard the various patristic statements in this matter to be pointers towards an even more profound understanding of recapitulation than a three-dimension working out of the doctrine will allow. Recapitulation, the gathering up of all things with humanity at their centre and as their raison d'être, in Christ, is not a matter of something accomplished at a given time within a time line as we know it. Certainly from our side within the dimension of our existence characterised by that time line, there is an historical event which we call the incarnation. But this is also an event beyond history, standing as the source of the beginning and continuance and end of that history. That source is that new beginning in God, whereby – not in the sense of any time sequence, for that cannot be projected into the existence of God – but in an ineffable and incomprehensible way to us, God becomes what He was not – Creator as well as Father.

In other words, God 'makes room' – and again not in the sense of measurable space, for that cannot be projected into the existence of God – for creation. And this 'making room' means his assuming to himself the cost of creating such an entity in its own integrity and freedom in its temporal/spatial dimension by recapitulating it from the beginning as the Word made flesh. We may interpret the fulness of the doctrine of recapitulation to be that all that we call this dimension of space is 'already' begun, 'present', summed up, and fulfilled at that beginning of creation, the source and perfector of which is the Word made flesh, in whom *the end is joined to the beginning*. Here is that Contingency of the humanity of Christ, for which God has 'made room' in his own Being, as the source of the contingency which is the nature of all created things. Space, which characterises the created dimension, is contingent to and from that Contingency within the existence of God.

Space, therefore, in theological terms, is a matter of relational quality to that which gives it existence. It is contingent to and from that, and therefore the question of infinity does not arise. Its assessment in its quality as that which, by the creative recapitulation of all things and all time accomplished by the Word made flesh, is dynamically present to God in its totality, does.

That is not to say that theology should dismiss the concept of infinity as having no use whatsoever. No doubt, mathematically, it is a convenience and a necessity as a theory. But metaphysically or ontologically used it is to be questioned. Theology can only know one Infinity, and that is God. But this Infinity is itself qualitatively other than any metaphysical infinity that could be deduced by the human mind. Indeed, as with any other attribute of God we use, it is questionable, for it implies 'endlessness' in a three-dimensional connotation. God is without such.

Certainly he is without beginning or end as he exists as Father, Son and Holy Spirit. The Beginning in God of which we spoke above is not a matter of God's nature, but of God's grace. It is the Beginning in which the beginning of creation, and therefore of space and time, depends and is brought about 'instantaneously'. But to say that God in his Triune existence is without beginning and without end, and therefore Infinite, does not imply that he exists as other things exist which have a beginning and an end – namely as a three-dimensional being without constriction of start and finish.

The term 'Infinite' as applied to God has to be emptied of all its created content; it is to be construed in such a radical way that it is seen to question all our supposed infinities.

This has always been an awareness in theology. Robert Grosseteste looked at the question of God and infinity in terms of god as the Mathematician, but in order to put mathematics in its context[25].

> *Sicut enim que vere in se finita sunt nobis sunt infinita, sic que vere in se sunt infinita, illi sunt finita. Iste autem omnia creavit in numero, pondere et mensura, et iste est mensurator primus et certissimus. Iste numeris infinitis, sibi certo et finito mensuravit et numeravit lineam cubilem, et numero infinito duplo lineam bicubilem et numero infinito subduplo lineam semicubilem.*

> For just as those things which in fact are finite in themselves, and to us they are infinite, so things which in fact are infinite in themselves are finite to Him. Moreover, He created all things in number, weight and measure, so He is the prime and most certain Mathematician. He, by infinite numbers, finite to Himself, measured the lines which He created. By means of some infinite number, to Him fixed and finite, He measured and numbered a line of one cubit, by a double infinite number a line of two cubits and by a half infinite number a line of half a cubit.

What Grosseteste is saying here is that all our infinities are finite to God, and that God works and measures in a way which is not discernible to, or understandable by, any means of human computation. It is noteworthy that Grosseteste never refers to God as infinite.

Long before Grosseteste we find the same treatment of the term infinite in its relation to God. Augustine of Hippo commented[26]:

> Far be it from us ... to doubt that all number is known to Him 'whose understanding' according to the Psalmist 'is infinite'. The infinity of number, though there be no numbering of infinite numbers, is yet not incomprehensible by Him whose understanding is infinite. And thus, if everything which is comprehended is comprehended or made finite by the comprehension of him who knows it, then all infinity is in some ineffable way made finite to God, for it is comprehended by His knowledge.

Three points emerge from the above quotations; that what we call infinities are relative within the created dimension:

that the concept 'infinity' is a comment on the limitations of the mind rather than a reality: and that God is over and above and beyond any supposed infinity.

Irenaeus too emphasises the radical nature of the infinitude of God as opposed to our infinities and perfections[27]:

> For this is the property of the working of God, not merely to proceed to the infinitude of the understanding, or even to overpass [our] powers of mind, reason and speech, time and place and every age; but also to go beyond substance, and fulness, or perfection.

Hilary of Poitiers likewise, in speaking of the works of God can say that[28]:

> ... the work of the Infinite and Eternal can only be grasped by an infinite intelligence.

And again, in speaking of any attempt in the temporal/spatial dimension to speak of infinity and the eternal begetting of the Son by the Father[29]

> Who surpasses by the eternity of His own infinity things which themselves are prior to earth and mountains and hills ... The voice of God ... teaches the absolute truth when it teaches that itself is not merely prior to things of time, but even to things infinite.

Infinity, then, theologically, can only be reserved for God, and it bears no resemblance whatsoever to any mathematical or metaphysical infinity which we may invoke. It revokes any such, for it is qualitatively different.

It is this Infinite, beyond and other than our projected infinities, which gives a beginning to finitude. But this relation is not one that can be understood other than in terms of the dynamic relations between the existence of the Creator and the existence of creation with humanity at its heart. This, as we have been stressing, is centred on the assumption of the flesh by the Word, in whom this relation is worked out in his recapitulation of all things, whereby they are held constant in their contingency to and from him by his grace and loving kindness, beginning, safeguarding, upholding, and perfecting, their freedom as created entities, and making room for them in maintaining their relation as finite things to the Infinite life of the Trinity.

But what may we say of the relation between the finite and this Infinite in terms of a dynamic existence? Here I wish to turn to the concept of light, for we are concerned in this question with the relation of God, as Uncreated Light and Rationality, and creation, as a creation of created light and rationality. We make entrance into this in a consideration of the remarkable work by Robert Grosseteste (c1170–1253), *De Luce*.

7

Space and Light

GROSSETESTE's treatise *De Luce* provides an insight into a theologian's endeavours to interpret the basis of creation, having regard to the nature of created realities as they are in themselves. This endeavour is best served by setting out Grosseteste's way of interpreting this in the order in which he does so.

He is concerned with the related themes of the creation of light, its character and behaviour, its relation to God, its place in the total work of creation and the subsequent nature of that creation.

The date of the treatise De Luce.
The composition of this short work may be dated between 1235–1241. The mature and reflective nature of its contents suggest that it is a later rather than, as Professor James McEvoy advocates[1], an earlier work. Sir Richard Southern stands by this later date on the grounds of the evolution in Grosseteste's thinking from the level of the understanding he had achieved by the time of the writing of the *Hexaemeron*. *De Luce*, in Southern's view[2], even if

> it tails away into a rather chaotic and unintelligible sequel in its final paragraphs

yet is

> one of the most lucid and brilliantly conceived pieces of writing of Grosseteste's later years.

The *Hexaemeron* he would date at 1232–1233. He sees a development in Grosseteste's ideas about light from its

> more confused and incomplete

treatment in the Hexaemeron, via its

> tentative form

in *De Operationibus Soli*, to its full fruition in De Luce[3].

McEvoy, on the other hand, argues that the more superficial treatment of light in the *Hexaemeron* and *De Operationibus Soli* is not due to undeveloped thought, but their having different and more limited purposes and objectives.

Southern counters this by showing the likelihood of Grosseteste repeating himself in the same way by which he uses material (among other instances) from his *Commentary on the Psalms* in the *Hexaemeron*. If De Luce was earlier, he had an already made work on light from which he would have been likely to take material for the *Hexaemeron*, either quoting it or summarizing it. There is not one hint of this. Moreover, such a work on all creation would have taken stock of the importance of light, as set out in *De Luce*, in the creative act.

There is no doubt that *De Luce* reflects a surer grasp and stronger understanding of the subject of light. Grosseteste states his findings definitively, and, while some Aristotelian terms are used, these are not the conveyors of Aristotelian substance of thought, but rather they are bent out of their accustomed philosophical usage to serve what is Grosseteste's originality of thought.

For example, the basic point of divergence between Aristotelianism and the thought expressed here is that matter is not pure potency for Grosseteste, but possesses innately a primordial, simple reality. Or again, his statement that there is

> a first bodily form, which some call corporeity

introduces a decidedly non-Aristotelian doctrine of a plurality of forms. The general method and presentation of this work is decidedly unscholastic and free of any Aristotelian shackles. For overall there is a method of thinking κατὰ φύσιν, that is to say, an objective way of thinking which does not approach the object of its study with preconceptions thereby subsuming the truth of the object to the mind's autonomy, but which allows the object from what it is in itself to inform the mind and conform the processes of the mind to its objective nature. And this despite the apparent emphasis on mathematical analysis.

This process of objective thinking evolves in Grosseteste's writings and is found in fully developed form in *De Luce*. It is an observational way of thought, but not one of mere surface observation. Rather it grapples with the totality of the nature of the object, in this case light, seeking to allow it to reveal itself by the mind's obedient perception to it as it really is in itself.

The precise setting out of his argument with all certainty and clarity displays a mind taking its own path with confidence. Such confidence is not evidenced in the more tentative approach to the subject of light in both the other works – *De Operationibus Soli* somewhat less hesitating than the *Hexaemeron*, but nevertheless still less definitive than *De Luce*.

De Luce seems to represent a final stage both in Grosseteste's way of thinking in general, his method of approach to the object of his study, and in the progression in particular of his exploration of light, its role in creation, its nature and its properties. On these grounds, Southern's dating of this as a more mature and developed theological and scientific work is preferable.

The scope of the Treatise.
The first section is bounded by the phrase at the beginning and repeated at the close

> *Formam primam corporalem.*

> The first bodily form.

In it, the nature and properties of light are succinctly set out. The instantaneous and omnidirectional diffusion of light is emphasised and its role in this action with regard to matter to which it is inseparably bound as the first and most exalted corporeal form. Its excellence lies in the fact that it bears closer resemblance than anything else to those forms, the intelligences, which exist apart from matter.

The second section concerns the mathematics of this action of light. This is a most significant development in thought, for there is implied clearly an advanced concept of relative infinities. The requirement of infinite multiplication of a simple being – that is, first matter – is required if that simple being is to be 'actualized' – by which Grosseteste means 'extended'.

His employment of mathematical concepts, here and in his other writings, in looking at the doctrine of creation and all its attendant issues is noteworthy. But the mathematics are made to serve the κατὰ φύσιν end. This is a consistent theme of his, for, as he remarks of God[4]:

> *iste est mensurator primus et certissimus.*

> so He is the prime and most certain Mathematician.

In the *Commentaries in VIII Libros Physicorum Aristotelis*, the burden of his argument is that what is infinite to us is finite to God. This has fundamental implications for the view, here worked out mathematically, that there is, for creation, a contingent relation to and from God, Who is over and beyond all measurement but Who[5]

> *omnia creavit in numero, pondere et mensura.*

> created all things in number, weight and measure.

The third section concerns the shape and quality of all creation through this movement and diffusion of light, infinitely multiplying itself equally in all directions from its primordial and simple point, and extending matter with it in so doing. This, and Grosseteste's subsequent description of the universe in terms of his understanding, foreshadows what has come to be called the 'Big Bang Theory'. Likewise, in the matter of the respective density and rotation of the spheres created in and by this action of light, there is an embryonic suggestion of the principle of gravity. Again, the idea of levels of relative existence interpenetrating one another, so that the lower field depends on the higher, is set out.

> *Cum auem corpora inferiora participant formam superiorem corporum, corpus inferius participatione eiusdem formae cum superiore corpore est receptivum motus ab eadem virtut emotiva incorporali, a qua virtute motiva movetur corpus superius.*

> When however, the inferior bodies share in the form of the superior bodies, the inferior body, by sharing of this same form with the superior body is capable of motion by the same incorporeal motive virtue, by which motive virtue the superior body is moved.

All bodies are actualised and qualified as light is qualified in its procession of instant generation and multiplication of itself. Light is the bond and characteristic of all creation. Multiplicity emerges from its simplicity, diversity from its unity.

The fourth section undoubtedly appears awkward and difficult, but if it is placed in the context of all that Grosseteste says about light and the firmament, the first or highest body of creation, then the logic in his thought here perhaps can be grasped. He wrote of the status of light in the *Hexaemeron*[6]:

> *Quapropter Deus, qui lux est, ab ipsa luce cuius tanta est dignitas merito inchoavit sex dierum opera.*

> Wherefore God, Who is light, by that selfsame light which assuredly is the dignity of all things, laid the foundation of the six days' work.

Here we have the view that light is created in correspondence to the uncreated Light of God: it is the order of all creation, the harmony of the universe, the beauty of nature, the perfection of art and the dignity of things seen and unseen.

Light (lux) from its primordial point extends, taking matter with it, to its rarified extreme. This, in the action of light instantly multiplying itself in three dimensions, is a sphere which is the first and highest body. This sphere reflects light (lumen) inwards and as it proceeds inwards in increasing density with matter, it creates the second sphere, inside which it, by like reflection, creates the third, and so on, until its extremity of density is reached.

The highest body, the firmament, is perfect. This section seems to be an attempt to analyse what constitutes perfection and unity in diversity, both for the simplest body, the first body, the firmament

> *in quo scilicet virtualiter cetera corpora sunt.*

> in which, that is, all other bodies are present virtually.

and for all other bodies contained in the subsequent spheres, down to the sphere of earthly elements. With this in view, while Grosseteste doubtlessly rounds off his treatise in the accepted contemporary manner of speculation on the perfect number, this is no mere stylistic finish demanded by custom. It is an attempt to portray all that has gone before with regard to light as the ground of perfection and the foundation of the stability of existence as it really is in itself in the creative intent of God.

The Sources behind De Luce

Only one source is explicitly mentioned in the Treatise – Aristotle's *De Caelo*, and to the section I:5–7 of that work appeal is made. However, Grosseteste's observations on light, while they may be set out in a unique way with original thought, are by no means the first on the subject. Behind him there is a hinterland of patristic and earlier mediaeval references to the subject, amongst the latter, for example, Anselm's *Proslogion* from the 11th century. It is probable that Grosseteste gathered up what was already familiar to him, but interpreted the significance of light in his own novel way with considerable insight peculiar to himself.

One of the main patristic authors on the subject of light was John Philoponos. No mention is made of this 6th century Alexandrian thinker by Grosseteste, but he may well have had cognition of that theologian's work on light via two sources: the books of patristic proof texts, such as the *Liber Scintillarum,* which compendiums usually had no reference to the original authors, and the works of the Islamic commentators such as Averroës and Avicenna, who certainly knew the works of Philoponos. The west in general knew little of the early Fathers of the eastern church, save through what Latin translations there were (and some of them indifferent to a precise rendering of the original Greek texts).

Grosseteste himself was a major influence in returning to such texts in their original tongue, even employing Greek servants to teach him, but he manifestly did not deal with any of Philoponos's works directly.

However, his comments on light and his method of approach to its significance in creation doubtlessly have a patristic influence. Indeed, the parallelism to Philoponos's thought is remarkable and merits serious research. Apart from this there is the general influence of Pseudo-Dionysius, with whose works Grosseteste was familiar and on which he commented. Here there is no explicit reference or immediate juxtaposition of overt Dionysian thought, but doubtless the familiarity with these works (though not uncritical) exercised a general influence.

There is, however, no hint whatsoever of the 'mysticism' of the supposedly Apostolic author – a facet of Pseudo-Dionysius with which Grosseteste would have little in common in any case by virtue of his essentially empirical way of thinking. This is clear in his commentaries on Pseudo-Dionysius's the *Divine Names*, the *Celestial Hierarchy* and the *Mystical Theology*, in which his own thoughts are outlined in addition to the disciplined commenting on the actual texts before him. The vision of God, for example, which the blessed see, is not, for Grosseteste, in terms of an ascension of appreciation through intermediaries, but is the direct knowledge of God as He is in Himself, *sine symbola et parabola* – *without symbol and parable*.

We turn to comment on other significant sections of the text of *De Luce*.

> *Formam primam corporalem, quam quidam corporeitatem vocant, lucem esse arbitror.*
>
> The first bodily form, which some call corporeity, I deem to be light.

Corporeity at creation is a simple substance, lacking all dimension. So is matter. It must be underlined here that although Grosseteste writes of them as two entities, he does not mean that they can exist independently of each other. He does not allow the possibility of regarding and examining them separately.

Matter, of and by itself, as a primordial point at creation, cannot effect anything. It is unproductive, impotent: of and by itself of no moment for the evolution of creation. *Simple substance* is rather a term which, given the development of matter in its full existence, is read back by Grosseteste from this present state of matter as a convenient theory to set out the nature of the first act of creation and the process involved thereafter.

Moreover, although he treats light or corporeity and matter as theoretically separate, it is the union of the two –

first form and first matter which is significant. For he looks at light also as a simple substance, devoid of dimension, but instantly and infinitely dynamic.

It may be noted here that Grosseteste's general scheme of calculation concerning infinities, set out in the second section of *De Luce*, is entirely in accord with what he examines here concerning those substances which have no dimension. The mathematics of infinity on the one hand are the same as those which would hold for simplicity on the other. The macroscopic and the microscopic aspects of the universe are an essential unitary field. It is to be noted that 'finite' and 'infinite' are restricted to the created dimension. 'Infinite' is never applied to God, nor is our way of mathematics God's way of mathematics.

The word *simple* requires elucidation. By this, Grosseteste means that it is uncomplicated by anything other than that it is in itself. It is of such fundamental essence that it has no weight, dimension or attribute other than that of a point – that is, with place but no measurement.

One suspects that we are at the frontiers of the adequacy of linguistic expression, and while it is necessary to go farther, the mind may turn around and around the concept, but should recognize the dilemma in encompassing these concepts in words and resist the temptation to so encapsulate them. Rather it must continue on its circuit and construct indicators rather than conclusions.

The implicit mathematics in this case is that a simple substance of no dimension plus another simple substance of no dimension will merely make one composite substance of primal corporeity and primal matter, still simple and of no dimension. This point is of great significance. For it means that the singularity at creation is corporeity and matter together, not separately.

> ... *cum non possit ipsa forma materiam derelinquere, quia non est separabilis, neo potest ipsa materia a forma evacuari*

> ... since form itself is not able to abandon matter, because it is not separable, nor can matter itself be emptied of form.

Primal corporeity (or first form) in its particular essence and primal matter are inextricably one. It would miss the significance of this to question whether or not matter pre-existed corporeity; whether there existed matter first and then corporeity was conjoined with it later. This presupposes that Grosseteste thought only in terms of linear time, and this is not necessarily the case. I believe that he was moving towards the idea of an 'instant' creation[7], whereby all things are present to God, all time being a dynamic present with God at creation. Here in Grosseteste's assertion that matter and form cannot exist without each other there is an indication that he assumes a simultaneous creation of form and matter in the one composite simple primal point.

Despite his observations variously on light and matter as simple substances, light and matter seem to be one and the same, for he afterwards treats matter only in terms of light and light only in terms of the purest matter.

Corporeity is the first form of creation. *Form* does not indicate 'shape' or 'surface contours'. It indicates 'dynamic order' or 'ordered energy'. Corporeity, as the first form created, is itself the order and movement of all matter. It is more than 'potential', for it is realized potential in its nature and action and, only as this, the shape of things. It is creative and ordered and ordering energy. That which alone has such a nature and action is, in Grosseteste's analysis and estimation, light.

Only light as it is in itself and no subsequent (and therefore lower and less perfect) form, could accomplish such order and movement. For:

> *Lux vero omnibus rebus corporalibus dignioris et nobilioris et exellentioris essentiae est*

> Light is of a more dignified, noble and excellent essence than all corporeal things.

Created light corresponds more closely to the pure and spiritual intelligences which are totally apart from matter. It is not an extension of uncreated Light (which can only be God Himself), or a 'form' (in the Aristotelian sense) of it. It corresponds to uncreated Light in its own created nature, and is thereby contingent to that uncreated Light, for it depends upon it for its creation and existence, and contingent from it, in that it is not that uncreated Light but is given its own nature and identity and quality as the prime created entity by that Light.

> *Quapropter Deus, qui lux est, ab ipsa luce cuius tanta est dignitas merito inchoavit sex dierum opera.*

> Wherefore, God Who is light, by that selfsame light which assuredly is the dignity of all things, laid the foundation of the six days' work[8]

At creation light is inseparably related to matter to which it gives dynamism and order of its union with it. That which by its nature, property and quality, gives dimension, direction, movement and achieving order with regard to matter, can alone be corporeity or light.

> *Corporeitas vero est, quam de necessitate consequitur extensio materiae secundum tres dimensiones.*

> Certainly corporeity is that which the extension of matter into three dimensions necessarily attends.

Grosseteste is deducing here that only in union with corporeity or light can matter be extended into three dimensions from its created point at which it has no dimension. Only light, which by nature multiplies and diffuses itself instantly in every direction, can be the agent and the reality of such an extension.

> *Lux enim per se in omnem partem se ipsam diffundit, ita ut a puncto lucis sphaera lucis quamvis magna subito generetur, nisi obsistat umbrosum.*

> For light spreads itself in every direction by itself, so that a sphere of light, however great you will, is generated instantly from a point of light, unless a cover obstructs.

In its union with matter light draws matter inseparably with it in its movement, and determines quality, disperses in quantity and orders all things in relation one to another, to the totality of them and to itself.

The implication here is that light is itself mobility and order, not merely the bestower of it – and is bracketed profoundly and inextricably together with life, that is with action, movement, direction, vivyfying. In other words it is essentially energy. This is its essential being. It bestows itself to that with which it is conjoined, so that in union with it, it participates in what light is and is characterized by it.

It begins as a point. Grosseteste describes light conjoined to matter of which it is the *form*, the dynamic order, at its creation as *simple*. That is to say, primordial light and primordial matter has no dimension. This means that we have in this conjunction of first light and first matter what may be called a 'singularity' composed as a point with place, but no dimension.

Instantly light diffuses itself in every direction until it reaches that distance where it is so rarifed that its movement ceases. In this action it draws matter, of which it is the dynamic order, along with it. The distance it travels in every direction forms a perfect sphere. The outer edge of this sphere, its circumference, at which no further movement can take place, is the firmament in Grosseteste's view.

This has much bearing on Grosseteste's concept of infinity. It will be noted that the infinite movement of light in every direction from its primordial point has a limit.

Only light could bring about this infinite and omnidirectional movement, thus extending matter and giving it dimension.

> *Formam vero in se ipsa simplicem et dimensione carentem in materiam similiter simplicem et dimensione carentem dimensionem in omnem partem inducere fuit impossibile, nisi ...*

> But it would be impossible for a form that is itself simple and devoid of dimension, to bring dimension in every direction into matter, similarly simple and devoid of dimension unless ...

Unless, of course, it were light, which alone has this property. It cannot even be another factor participating in the power of light, for this would be a form secondary to light, and it is impossible for a primary form to introduce dimensions into matter via a secondary or derivative form. That would be to compound its simplicity and deny the singularity of the creation of light.

In this way Grosseteste concludes that light is the first corporeal form; it is not a form following from corporeity, but is corporeity itself. All creation therefore is typified by light. It is a creation of light.

Behind this there may lie the desire to demonstrate that creation is a matter of contingency to and from God; that it is brought into being out of nothing by an act of sheer grace, and corresponds in its created dimension as a creation of light, to the uncreated rationality which God, as uncreated Light, is. For something other than light – even if it participates in the power of light – to bestow dimension and direction and order, removes the direct, determinative priority of light from creation, and hints covertly at a dualism of matter and light.

Just as creation is a direct act of God himself, without the aid of any emanations as co-creators to assist in the work, so the order of creation is not a matter of emanated gradation as to its substantive nature, one created order dependent on another higher one for its existence. It is a unity of light within the ordering of which gradation takes place in accordance with that unity and the nature of light.

This is borne out by the insistences characterizing Grosseteste's doctrine of creation of the distinction between, yet the relation of, Creator and creation. The same refrain is found throughout his theological works, that creation is a creation *ex nihilo*. Nothing exists beside God, who in his Triune Being is all sufficiency, all company, all majesty, needing nothing, with no compulsion from without to create, no necessity from within. Creation, in short, is an act of God's free grace. God creates in accordance with his nature; that is, there is a correspondence between God as uncreated Rationality and the rationality of the created dimension. Creation is not an extension of God, but in its qualitative difference as created, it corresponds to that Rationality which he is in himself. Grosseteste everywhere sees such a mirror of the Trinity in the forms and nature of created realities. In speaking about sight and light[9] he writes:

> *Hec itaque tria Trinitatis exampla est invenire universaliter in omnibus. Inter res autem corporeas manifestissimum Trinitatis exemplum est ignis, sive lux, que necessario de se gignit splendorem; et hec due in se reflectunt mutuum fervorem. In coniunctione autem corporei cum incorporeo,*

prima exampla sunt in formis sensibilibus, et speciebus formarum sensibilium generatis in sensibus, et intentione animi coniungente speciem genita in sensu cum forma gignente que est extra sensum. Et huius rei evidentior est examplacio in visu. Color enim rei colorate gignit de se speciem sibi similem in oculo videntis; et intencio animi videntis coniungit speciem coloris genitam in oculo cum colore gignente exterius; et sic unit gignens et genitum quod apprehensio visus non distinguit inter speciem genitam et colorem gignentem; fitque una visio ex gignente et genito et intencione copulante genitum cum gignente. Et similiter est ista trinitas in quolibet exteriorem sensuum.

Thus, therefore, there are three examples of the Trinity to be found universally in everything. Amongst bodily things the most manifest example of the Trinity is fire, or light, which by necessity begets splendour from itself, and these two reflect their mutual warmth. However, in conjunction of the bodily with the incorporeal, the prime examples are in forms apprehended by the senses and in species of sensible forms generated in the senses, and by the intent of the mind the species begotten in the sense is yoked with the begetting form which is outside the sense. However the most evident example of these things is in the sight. For the colour of a thing begets as coloured the species similar to itself in the eye of the beholder; and the intention of the viewing mind conjoins the species begotten of colour in the eye with the external begetting colour; and thus begetter unites with begotten, because the apprehension of the sight does not distinguish between the begotten species and the begetting colour; and there is made one vision out of the begotten by the deliberate embrace of the begetter with the begotten. And this Trinity is similar in any exterior sense.

Here we have a very subtly worked out analogy to the Trinity, to the Father (the Begetter), the Son (the Begotten) and the embracing bond of the Holy Spirit uniting them. Analogous to the Trinity in the created dimension are the constituent parts involved in the operation of light and the mind. These are: the object observed, the image of that object in the mind, and the process of the mind informed by light whereby the external image and the internal image perceived in the mind are joined as one.

What also is noteworthy here is the propriety of language – begetting and begotten and the embrace of unity, all of which are adhered to consistently and extended as the analogy processes.

Moreover, here there is a declaration of objectivity as the necessary ground of knowledge and the obedience of the mind in imaging that objective verity. Only thus comes about the integrity of knowledge.

There are plenty of other examples of Trinitarian analogies throughout Grosseteste's works – from the speck of dust[10] (*atomus* is the word he uses which may reflect Philoponos's often found usage of ἄτομος) to the incomprehensible magnitude of the action and nature of light.

All this is not some form of 'Natural Theology' whereby God can be read off the face of nature instantly, automatically and mechanically. For his doctrine of the Trinity is taken only from the self-revelation of God, the Word, one with the Father in the bond of eternal love the Holy Spirit, made flesh, as the Triune God.

It is to and from this God in all his self-sufficient majesty, that creation is contingent. The relation of the creation to its Creator is exemplified in that Word made flesh, Jesus Christ, where the Creator confronts us in all his divinity as one of his own creatures with this flesh and nature of ours. Herein is exhibited that which gives unity to all creation, the Creator taking his own to himself.

Behind this lies a perception which Gosseteste never states explicitly, but towards which he may have been moving, of the necessary unity between the act of Creation and the Incarnation. This I have developed fully in *The Anachronism of Time*, and here only indicate that in my view the rationale of creation and the temporal/spatial entities thus brought into being, can only be understood if the principle of creation is Incarnation.

That is to say, that creation and Incarnation are the two sides of the one will, decree and act of God, by whom all time is embraced in its beginning, continuance, end and fulfilment, as a dynamic present. If it is otherwise, then we can only deem God to be contingent upon time as the hapless victim of what He has unwittingly unleashed at creation and having to undertake a rescue exercise by the Word made flesh at a later date. This spawns and projects all manner of

spatial and temporal problems into questions about the relation between Creator and creation, and we end up with dealing with the issue by trying to solve it by three-dimensional
absurdities.

If creation and incarnation are so bound together, the first
brought about on the basis of the latter, then this both safe-
guards the freedom of creation as an entity distinct from God
with its own identity and nature and quality, and yet
contains the effect of that freedom which cannot support
itself within dependency upon the sustaining grace of God.
This is a statement of that which is implicit in Grosseteste's
thought of the principle of double contingency: that creation
is utterly dependent upon God for its beginning, continuance, upholding and fulfilment – its contingency TO God –
yet is given by the grace of God its own dimension, identity,
nature, which is other than His qualities – its contingency
FROM God.

Grosseteste's question[11] as to whether or not the Incarnation would have taken place if there had not been a 'fall' of
humanity, and his answer in the affirmative, demonstrates
his view that the Incarnation is profoundly bracketed with
creation and indeed is the principle of it. This is further
enlarged upon by his assertion that the only unifying principle of all temporal and spatial realities is the fact, event and
Person of the Word made flesh, where these created realities
are recapitulate in the relation of the humanity of Christ to
His divinity.

But this all follows the same pattern of what he regards as
the place of light in the cosmos. Light is that which characterises everything that has been made both as these things are
in themselves and as they exist in relation to other things.
Each level of existence is bound to other levels, each field of
activity to other fields, by light. On the temporal/spatial level
only, light is also the unifying factor in all creation, for it is
the first corporeal form from which all else comes through its
behaviour and activity. The implicit sum of Grosseteste's
commentary on light is that light is the recapitulation of all
things. But created light is and does this only because it
corresponds in its created nature to that Uncreated Light
which God is, and which the Nicene-Constantinopolitan

Creed relates to the Word in His relation with the Father – Light of Light. It is this Uncreated Light by whom all things are made, and made as a creation of light, corresponding in its light-determined rationality to the Uncreated Light and Rationality of God.

Although he does not openly state such, the logical conclusion of all that he is reaching towards in his analysis of creation as a creation of light is that all things and all time are gathered in that singularity of the first creation – the point of light. This would be, as it were, recapitulation in reverse, recapitulation at the beginning of creation. All time and all space are instantaneously present in that beginning which is the 'Let there be light'. All things are thereafter refracted into their constituent levels, existences and that order which we know as this temporal/spatial dimension.

But we are again faced with what this beginning of creation implies – that behind this beginning of creation lies a Beginning in God, and it is surely here that the unifying principle of all creation is found. Here we are confronted with the inadequacy of language to convey with all propriety what a 'Beginning' in God means.

By it I do not mean that there is a time before time, a beginning before the beginning of creation. That would be to construe God as existing in time, even if this is perceived to be some sort of 'endless' time. It is the very fact that time begins with creation, that creation is not made in time but that time is co-created with existence as its necessary character, which causes our inadequacy of language. We can only speak in time with the restrictions of time constraining us. Our language is time-bound.

Athanasius poses the dilemma to which we come in saying that creation has a beginning[12]:

> Therefore the creatures began to be made; but the Word of God, not having beginning of being, certainly did not begin to be, nor begin to come to be, but was ever. And the works have their beginning in their making, and their beginning precedes their coming to be; but the Word, not being of things which come to be, rather comes to be the Framer of those which have a beginning.

Athanasius is countering the Arian claims that the Word was

the first of all creatures by insisting on His co-eternity and consubstantiality with the Father. The beginning in God does not consist in the claim that there was a time when the Word was not – the Arian maxim – but it does consist in the fact that the Word *comes to be the Framer* of creation, which office and work He did not have 'before'. God was 'always' Father, Son and Holy Spirit, but 'now' (that is, in the act of creating) He 'becomes' what He was not 'before', namely Creator as well as Father. But we must not posit a time scale for this 'becoming', this 'beginning' in God. Rather, all we may say is that as the Triune God exists as the three Persons 'making room' for each other in that ineffable non-spatial existence, so God 'makes room' for this activity of His which means that He 'becomes' Creator also.

In so doing, He makes room for His creation, which in its room or space, corresponds in its created dimension to the 'room' which the Persons of the Godhead make for each other and for their creative love. Space then is the particular way in which creation exists, as existences in all their diversity held together in their relations one to another and all to each, as the created correspondence to the 'space' which God has within His own being to be the Triune Creator God He is.

But this God exists in this non-spatial, non-temporal way, in relation to what He has created out of nothing. I would suggest that we can only perceive that all time and all space, that is to say, all things which are brought into being and have time and space as their creative characteristic because they are existences other than God, are 'present', 'instantaneously', to God.

This being the case, as has already been stated, Incarnation and Creation are 'instantaneous' to God. The Incarnation is not a Divine afterthought, a mere rectifying of creation, but is the very cost borne by God in creating. The beginning of creation is also its end, its totality and its fulfilment, from the side of God. It is created to share His divine life which it does by the fact that God grasps to His very own being its being in incarnation.

Space and time, that which we experience as the room of the expression of our existence, is the refraction of that which is dynamically present to God in its totality in His Word. It is by the Word made flesh that all things are created. The groaning and travailing of all creation, of which St Paul speaks[13], is the created dimension's participation in the cost of God creating, which He bears in His Word. Crucifixion and Resurrection are writ large in every element and atom, as the refraction of that recapitulation whereby all time and space is present to God in His Word, that Word which declares 'let there be' and becomes flesh in that becoming of creation.

Our refracted light, the light which makes us what we are and gives us in that nature space and time which we measure out in its finite vastness, is but our creaturely perception and working out of that new beginning in God wherein the end is joined to the beginning. The totality of space and time is as a single beam of light in that 'infinity' of Uncreated Light which God is.

8

Space and Place

SPACE – the room occupied by the universe, even if its vast-ness surpasses our capability of measuring it, and we thereby fall back on that excuse for our limitations, the concept of infinity – is the freedom which God gives creation to be itself. Within that grant of God, creation makes room for itself. Its existence as the totality of all existences composing it and making room for themselves in their essential integrities and in their relation one to another, creates space.

But this is to be perceived as the nature of what creation is and what it has as its own. Space (and time) are confined to creation. There is no space or time apart from the created realities. We cannot ask 'Where is creation?' We can only say 'It is in its own place'. We cannot ask 'Where is God?' But we cannot say, as of creation, that he is in his place. The existence of God is qualitatively other than existence characterised by time or space. But he is not related to time and space negatively. He is the bestower of time and space because He creates that which is other than himself. These are the especial marks of created existence. They are peculiar to it. God is not so, as Gregory of Nyssa pointed out[1]:

> The Divine nature is a stranger to these special marks of creation. It leaves beneath itself the sections of time, the 'before' and the 'after', and the ideas of space: in fact 'higher' cannot properly be said of it at all.

This is behind Grosseteste's observations on light and creation as a creation of light. Light, from its initial point, expands in every direction, making room, by its activity of rarefaction ordering and placing matter of which it is the purest form. But this is created light in its distinction from the Uncreated Light which God is. The activity of created light gives room for each created existence and entity, and relates them, in their respective orders, one to another and binds them together as a created totality.

Vast as this created totality might be, he observes, all the supposed infinities which we ascribe to it are but finite to God who is alone Infinite.

The Infinity of God is not endless time or immeasurable space. It is true Infinity because it comprehends, apprehends and gathers together the totality of all things that are created. If we say that it encloses them, that does not mean in an Aristotelian sense that we regard God as a vast container. Rather, it means that there is a relation of existences of an utterly different quality, the Uncreated and Creator related to the created, his creature.

This relation does not admit of mathematical resolution. It is not quantitive, it is qualitive. 'Infinity', if we use the term of God, must be shorn of all its mathematical and creaturely trappings. It does not come within our conceptual grasp, even as a postulated 'infinite'. Nor can it be perceived as this which is 'Wholly Other'. That in itself depends on the perception of that to which it is compared. Our dilemma is that we can only describe the totality and therefore the full character of that to which it is compared, namely all creation, in the light of that to which creation is related, namely God. The 'via negativa' way of approaching God has already been dealt with and rejected above.

This too is the dilemma of Pseudo-Dionysius, whose works so influenced many of the mediaeval theologians. In *The Divine Names* he discusses the propriety of naming God, that is, the difficulty of approaching God by way of positive knowledge. His solution is in effect to dismiss God as unknowable – and indeed he pays lip service to the incarnation as the Self-revelation of God, preferring to rise in a 'mysticism' whereby he is caught up in a cloud of unknowing and contemplates the God who is beyond all being.

This is summed up in his *The Mystical Theology*[2] where he, having said that the cause of all, that is the Word of God, is both eloquent and silent, is indeed *wordless*. That is, he interprets the Word as, even in His speaking being beyond words. This Word is found by those who, on a mystical pilgrimage, forsake every rational indication, whether from heaven or on earth, and pass into that darkness where God dwells. This is a reference to Moses ascending the mount to meet with God, and passing into the cloud of God's presence.

In fairness to that author known as Pseudo-Dionysius, it must be said that he has faced and grappled with the dilemma of the limitations of human language. But in so doing he construes God as being beyond all being, and that the perception whereby we know God is beyond rationality. He has taken the *via negativa* to its absurd conclusion, and we are left in the last resort with a vivid and vicious dualism between not just form and content, spiritual and material, heavenly and earthly, but between rationality and the knowledge of God.

It is in such soil that so much of what is now called 'mysticism' and 'spirituality' has taken odious and malignant root. 'Spirituality', as an exercise in itself, has the inherent danger of becoming an alternative to the discipline of theology, and a short cut to God by forsaking the necessity of wrestling with God's purpose for his created handiwork and his relation to it.

God is not wordless. He is his Word. That Word is the One by Whom all things were created. In his Word, God makes room for us, and gives us the freedom to make room for ourselves. Through his Word he orders all things. He administers οἰκονομία, the ordering of his household of creation. Within that ordering, in the relation which all the created entities have from each other and towards each other, he has given each its place. That is to say, he has respect for the integrity of each thing and level of existence which he has created.

He is Place, for he is the bestower of place for every constituent part of what he has brought into being, and on his Place all things depend. The existence of every thing depends on the existence of God. The place of every thing, which is the freedom of all the created realities to create space, depends on the God Who is Place, since he is the ground of all being, the Being on whom all being depends.

The space which the created entities make for themselves are their identities. They create space either in accordance with their relation to the Creator and therefore in accordance with what they really are in themselves in that light, or they create it in selfish self-assertion without regard to the One to Whom they are, in the first and last resort, related on whom they depend.

That there is chaos is the result of the tension between the contingency TO God, the utter dependence upon him, and the contingency FROM God, the freedom he bestows upon his creation as an entity other than himself with its own identity and nature. Chaos is the result of existences not creating the appropriate place which their nature demands, but overstretching themselves to be what they are not, by God-given nature, intended to be.

Place becomes a battleground of jockeying for self-perceived position and right. It becomes, in terms of human being, territorial, valued in quantity – existence measured in quantitive values. Space becomes that which is to be exploited in these terms.

Two points become obvious here. First: that the pain of existence and creation is caused by a breakdown between the contingency TO and the contingency FROM God. These go out of balance and eventually are fractured and parted the one from the other. Freedom is not construed as freedom towards God, but freedom away from God as self-expression, and therefore, because the fundamental context of individual existence is not appreciated, a disregard for the context within the created level of how all things are related one to the other and all to the Creator and a subsequent disparagement and manipulation or discarding of anything which is judged to be an obstruction to that self-fulfilment and self-expression.

This lies behind the failure of society to be properly social, and behind the callous exploitation of resources both natural and human. Place is not given — respect is not accorded.

Second: no doubt there is an equivalent to human ways of working in the natural order. There is tension in the created order between opposing forces in the whole evolutionary process. This chaos is the groaning and travailing of all creation. But if all this, and indeed human failings, are taken into account in the light of what has been said about the mode of God creating through incarnation, we can see that

God has taken stock of the cost of creation, and borne the vulnerability of its freedom by involving his very Being and taking that cost and pain upon himself in the Word made flesh.

For God to make room for an entity other than himself, which may participate in his divine life as its fulness and its true identity, is a matter of the Word being made flesh.

God makes room for all creation. He allows everything in the freedom which it has as that which is created to express itself in making its place. The totality of places, that is, existences, is the space that we perceive as we explore the whole of the universe in its macroscopic and its microscopic forms.

This means that the place we have for ourselves and which we make for ourselves, and the place which all the other orders of creation have and make, is the freedom he gives to us and to the natural forces, to be what we are in ourselves as he intended us to be. But this freedom comes in terms of the cost to God which he has taken to himself in the Word made flesh, that order may come out of chaos, that all things may be upheld in their courses despite waywardness, that all things may work together for good.

This can only be sought and known in the fact that God is not without his Word, through Whom he has given place for us, in Whom he has made all things to consist, and in Whom all things have their beginning and their fulfilment.

The totality of space is the interaction of that love of God in creating with what he has created. It is the place of his activity towards us, and our disposition towards him summed up in the Word made flesh. Space is the coinherence of all that God has created in its inner relativities and in its relation to its Creator.

One whose significance in the field of theology, in his insight into the awe and reverence towards the doctrine of creation, and the thankfulness of proper spirituality which this calls forth when it is viewed in the light of the Word made flesh, has been noted and advocated by A. M. Allchin. This is the seventeenth century theologian and parish priest, Thomas Traherne. A. M. Allchin has put before us – and it is hoped will further the process – something of much value in his little book of excerpts from Traherne's works, *Land-*

scapes of Glory. Reading this is a foil to the unanchored mysticism of Pseudo-Dionysius, for it reveals Traherne's – and hopefully our – appreciation of creation as the place of God's interaction with us in the material, the finite, the loved and the homely.

I lift but a few instances of Traherne's insight from A. M. Allchin's compendium[3], in the hope that it may prompt others to read Traherne more fully.

> You never enjoy the world aright, till the sea itself floweth in your veins, till you are clothed with the heavens, and crowned with the stars, and perceive yourself to be the sole heir of the whole world, and more than so, because men are in it who are every one sole heirs as well as you.
>
> Till you can sing and rejoice and delight in God, as misers do in gold and kings in sceptres, you never enjoy the world.
>
> Some things are little on the outside and rough and common. But I remember the time, when the dust of the streets was as precious as gold to my infant eyes, and now is more precious to the eye of reason.
>
> When we dote upon the perfections and beauties of some one creature, we do not love that too much, but other things too little.
>
> Never was anything in this world loved too much, but many things have been loved in a false way, and in all too short a measure.

Here there is summed up the reverence for creation, the awareness of which is described as the ordinary and humdrum, the place which each constituent part makes for itself, the wonderment of humanity for the work of God in rationality and humanity's perception of the openness of creation to God, Who embraces it all.

There is no recourse to mathematical infinities as a framework to describe all that exists. There is a glad and humble acceptance open to that which lies beyond on the created level and to that which gives it, in God's creative grace, through his Word, place and purpose, space and identity.

There is a further consideration; that of the relation between Creator and creation with regard to 'place'. We have looked already at this problem as it arose in terms of the incarnation, the Word making room for himself in his own creation, and making room for his creation in union with his divine existence. The resurrection and the ascension of our Lord heighten the meaning of this, for they are the climax of incarnation, the declaration of incarnation in purpose and fulfilment.

Incarnation, crucifixion, resurrection and ascension, the events of the involvement of the Word made flesh in the spatial/temporal dimension of creation, are to be seen as one movement, as facets of one event. Here we have to use language which must not be construed as indicating spatial content, as even the very word 'movement' might suggest. It is the 'movement' of the Creator taking to himself his creation in all its limitation and vulnerability. It is a 'movement' from beyond the boundaries of created existence, God rising out of his place, 'coming down' into them, taking them into union with himself and 'going up' into that 'beyond'. But that 'beyond' is not some conceptual infinite space or endless time. This movement is the event and proclamation whereby God makes room for himself in his creation and makes room for it in himself.

This is not to be construed in quantitative concepts – of a 'greater' being squeezed into a 'lesser' (the problem behind the Lutheran/Calvinist debate in the 17th century), or a 'lesser' being subsumed into the 'greater'. It is to be seen in terms of the relation of utterly different existences which in Christ are reconciled and harmonized and, in their respective integrities, made inseparable.

In considering above the relation between creation and incarnation, it was emphasised that the latter was the mode of the former. The idea that the incarnation was merely a divine afterthought subsequent to creation and the fall was questioned. If the incarnation is divorced from the act of creation in this way – which separation arises out of implicitly thinking that the incarnation is but God's act when he realised after a time that he had to do something about what he had set in being – then we have made God contingent upon time and the events in the temporal dimension, and can only construe from that that he exists in endless time, qualitatively no different from our temporal existence but only quantitatively so.

The relation between time and space being inseparable (we

existing in a space/time continuum) then God's existence must, on the basis of quantitative difference only from us, equally be one which is spatial.

We are then faced with questions which are absurd: 'Where is God'; 'What size is God?' It is in this implicit thinking about the incarnation being such a divine afterthought that unfortunate concepts of infinity and eternity arise, being brought in to attempt to answer the problems thrown up by this interpretation of a time lapse from the side of God between the act of creation and the event of the Word made flesh, and a spatial differential between Creator and creature.

That is why we also questioned these concepts of infinity and eternity as sought from an basis in the understanding of temporal and spatial concepts, and in so doing why we further rejected any reality of the mathematical/philosophical approach, however convenient this approach may be for theoretical mathematical computation. This approach is not to be transferred into an understanding of existence, God's or ours.

If any such concepts are so transferred, then a metaphysical or ontological/philosophical view which is firmly anchored in objective thought in appreciating the temporal/spatial realities as they are in themselves, can only treat 'infinity' and 'eternity' as conceits of our limited mental capacities straining to describe what cannot be described and therefore as comments on our incapacity to subsume the whole of creation within our understanding. 'Infinity' and 'eternity' are in the last analysis impudent concepts which betray our attempt to cloak that incapacity.

There may (though not in Aristotelian terms) be infinite possibilities within the complexity of the created order. I have not said 'infinite potential', for that phrase suggests an underlying infinity in all things finite. That there are infinite possibilities merely underlines our unawareness of the total comprehension of all things and their full significance, and the fact that more and more could be understood, but never the fulness of it all. Again, this is a comment on our insufficiency, not a statement of the nature of the totality of creation.

It has been underlined that we should not be concerned

with calculations of mathematical dimensions, but with the relations of different existences – God in his Uncreated Being and we, and all the created entity, in our and its bounded existence. We are therefore concerned with dynamic relations and not static concepts. Space is then seen to be that which is construed in terms of these dynamic relations, those which obtain within the complexity of the levels of existence within the created dimension and the totality of these in their relation to their Creator and his actions and existence.

I suggest that the whole event of incarnation, crucifixion, resurrection and ascension, is the interaction of the Being of God, as he creates, with what he has created. It is the cost to his Being, which, in overflowing love in creating an entity distinct from himself in its freedom to be the creation it is yet dependent upon him for its necessary upholding in existence, he himself bears. *The groaning and travailing* of all creation which St Paul notes[4], and that commented upon by John Calvin[5]:

> There is no element and no part of the world which ... is not intent on the hope of its resurrection

may be interpreted as the creation's participation in this act of bringing the universe into being through incarnation, whereby God bears the cost of creation, in the way in which that single 'instant' as a dynamic, fulfilled 'Now' on God's side, is refracted in the dimension of space and time.

Karl Barth, in his *Commentary on the Epistle to the Romans* expresses both the tension between the finite dimension of space and time, the existence of creation, and the Uncreated Existence of God, and the inseparable bond between them. It is to be noted that he does this with realism and not with the escapism of false piety. Such false piety, or *religion* as a discovery by humanity, has, for Barth, its counterpart in every attempt of secular human philosophy to adorn the creation with what is other than its frailty, mortality and limitations. Even if we think we do the awesomeness of the universe service by speaking of its infinity or its endlessness, we indulge in such delusion. It is finite, even if the extent of that finitude is more than we can bear or measure, and must not be confused with That which is truly

Infinite, because that That is God in his utterly distinctive existence. He comments on the eighteenth verse of the eighth chapter of *The Epistle to the Romans*[6].

> The writer does not, for example, redress the tribulation of the world by fixing our attention upon the compensating harmony of another world. No careless attitude to present tribulation can stand even before the aching of a tooth, and still less before the brutal realities of birth, sickness and death, before the iron reality which governs the broad motions of the lives of men and the stern destiny of nations. Beneath each slight discomfort, and notably beneath the greater miseries of human life, there stands clearly visible the vast ambiguity of its finiteness. How are we able to meet this? All our answers, all our attempts at consolation, are but deceitful short-circuits, for from this vast ambiguity we ourselves emerge; we cannot escape from it, not even if we invoke in our imaginings an infinite divine harmony beyond this world of ours. The infinity of our imagination is measured by our limitation and achieves no more than infinite-finiteness ... Not for some relative thing does the ambiguity of our finiteness cry out, but for the Absolute: it cries for an answer beyond our comprehension, for the true and Unknown God: it cries out for His consolation, with which the sufferings of this present time are not worthy to be compared, a consolation opposed to this present time as the immeasurable 'There' is opposed to the measurable 'Here'.

But when we apprehend the incarnation, crucifixion, resurrection and ascension of Christ as the action of God in his Self-revelation bridging this distinction between himself and his creation, then it is that we see and understand the dimension of this creation as

> the ocean of concrete, observable reality, in which the submarine island of the Now of divine revelation is altogether submerged but remains, nevertheless, intact, in spite of its shallow covering of observable things. This Now ... this Moment beyond all time, when men stand before God, this 'Point' from which we come, but which is no point in the midst of other points, Jesus Christ crucified and risen, – is the Truth.

It is this by this Moment that the existence of creation

> is measured and without which it would not exist.

The action of God in his divine existence grasping creation to himself is that from which we come and to which we go. This Self-revelation and Personal act of God, whereby creation and incarnation are inseparably bracketed together, is our vantage point from which all other things are measured. In that context, there is nothing before this which is infinite or eternal. All is relative in its finitude and its temporality to the One who alone is Infinite and Eternal in a way which is not merely and trivially space and time to the nth degree. The existence of God is not available to measurement or infinite concepts.

Throughout Barth's thought in his Commentary runs the utter distinction between Creator and creature. That abyss, by which he means *qualitative difference* cannot be bridged by any attempt from the side of creation. Any attempt to do so is only delusion; it is like the passionate attempt of Prometheus to steal the fire from Zeus, and yet in thinking that divine fire, which can never be seized, has been taken, the very human nature of that fire is obvious. It is used for humanity's own advantage as it sees its own good, and that is tragic delusion.

> ... is it not perfectly obvious that such stolen fire is not the all consuming fire of God, but only a furnace from which a very peculiar kind of smoke pours forth? ... Smoke from the fire of Zeus may penetrate farther than other fumes, it may display greater variety, but it does not differ in kind. In any case, it is not by the possession of such fire that we pass from death to life, or put an end to human passions. Rather, it is the crowning of all other passions with the passion of eternity, the endowment of what is finite with infinity ...[7]

While Barth is here attacking religiosity, and the false idea that religious perception and experience is the entrance to an understanding of eternity and infinity, this may also be applied to all human endeavour, and especially to philosophical endeavour, to penetrate what lies beyond the finite and the temporal. His point is that created existence is limited, frail and mortal. Any 'rising up' beyond such bounds both denies the essential nature of creation and provides an illusion as to what has been supposedly discovered in such rising up. All endeavour is finite and can deal only with the finite.

What is truly Infinite and Eternal is God alone and here is the radical otherness of Infinity as opposed to all finitude and the attempts to rise above that limitation which are but the extension of the finite.

The existence of the created, creation's place, has to be respected for what it is. No service is rendered to it by supposing that it can reach the infinite. A qualitative gulf is fixed so that we cannot pass over to God's 'Place', that is, perceive and know the existence of God as he is in himself. Only God can 'arise out of his place' and grasp the finite to himself.

The 'Place' of God, the room that he has made for himself as he exists as Father and Son bound in the bond of divine love, the Holy Spirit, is that which makes room for his creation. But they are not alike, these 'rooms'. The place of creation is not, of itself, the place of God. It is only the place of God, and therefore the creation it is intended to be, because God's place permits it its place and takes it into union with itself. The finite is thereby open to the Infinite – by the act of God's existence as the incarnate, crucified, risen and ascended Word. Of itself it is bounded, finite and temporal.

'Place' is determined by the particular nature and quality of that which makes it. It is existence and activity. If the existence and activity is of that which is created, then all created space – the totality of the places of creation – is finite. If the existence and activity is of that which is Uncreated – the Triune God existing in his Self-sufficiency – then it is Infinite. But the former cannot be turned into the latter by any endeavour of any creature. That would be to deny its essential being and disparage it.

> We know – not some concrete, visible, corporal divine thing! If that were the object of our knowledge, God would not be God. Men do not force their way into His Kingdom; nor is it projected into this world. To us God is the Stranger, the Other, whom we finally encounter along the whole frontier of our knowledge[8].

None of this is to be construed as the adoption of a pessimistic view of a creation of degradation. Far from it. On the contrary, it is the establishing of the integrity of creation, which integrity is found in a realistic look at the limitations of creation – its finitude and its temporality – and at the relation of these limitations to that from which and to which they are contingent. This contingency of creation would disappear if the universe is infinite and eternal, and that disappearance would include the vanishing of all rationality from its fabric, for that rationality is established upon that very contingency.

An infinite universe would have no place. This means that it would not have discernible and rational existence. It is only as the space of creation, the totality of the places of the created entities, is seen to be related to that which gives it beginning, upholding and purpose, and open to that Place of the Creator which qualitatively is beyond all conception of space, that it has rationality and the possibility of perceiving the unfolding of its own finite wonders which are more than we can express.

Perhaps Barth's pointed comment on the matter of minds thinking that they are capable of stretching themselves towards the infinite and in that exercise in fact deal falsely with creation's nature, may serve as an epitaph to all such[9]:

> Once again we have to be reminded, lest we fall into some romanticism or other, how complex is our life on this side of the Resurrection. This way and that, our path is crossed by every kind of human possibility, high and low, noble and vulgar, significant and trivial. Art, science and morality display the passionate longing of men for infinity. Yes, but, God knows, we also hunger and thirst, we digest our food, and sleep, and lust. And where is the boundary line between the two? Can any one rid me of the suspicion, amounting almost to a certainty, that the story of my life and the history of humanity could be more honestly described if the stomach rather than the head were adopted as the point of departure?

So we are reminded of the corporeal limitations of creation, and therefore its nature and the quality of space as the totality of all the 'places' of the entities of which it is composed as these are in themselves and in their relations, their interactions and interlocking one with another.

I suggest that the whole event of incarnation, crucifixion, resurrection and ascension, is the interaction of the Being of

God as he creates with what he has created. It is the cost of his Being which, in overflowing love in creating an entity distinct from himself to share his divine life, without any necessity either internal or external upon him to do so, that he bears. The event of the Word made flesh is the travailing and pangs of God in bringing creation into existence as that which is inseparably but unconfusedly united with him that it may have its own integrity and freedom to be what it is, yet upheld and sustained and given fulfilment by him as it cannot of itself exist through itself, by itself and for itself.

It is in this Word made flesh that all things were

> created, in the heavens and upon the earth, things visible and invisible ... all things have been created through him, and unto him: and he is before and in him all things consist[10]. ... to sum up all things in Christ, the things in the heavens, and the things upon the earth[11].

But out of this claim of theology we have two other considerations to face with regard to space and place. The first concerns the nature of the movement of the ascension of Christ, the second the concept of 'heaven'.

These two are comprehended in the phrase *ascended into heaven*, and it is to a consideration of the implications of that phrase with regard to space and place that we now turn.

9

'Ascended into Heaven'

ASCENSION and heaven are interlinked, for it is from 'heaven' that the Word 'descends' and to 'heaven' that he 'ascends'. We have already stated that such credal statements as *came down from heaven ... ascended into heaven, And sitteth on the right hand of the Father* cannot be interpreted spatially, as if the Word came on some cosmic journey from a higher sphere to a lower one. And we have discussed already the 'downward' movement of the Word made flesh, as the interaction of the divine existence of the One by whom all things were made with the existence of what is created as it is created.

Resurrection and ascension are the 'upward' movement within that same event of that same Word made flesh, establishing that interaction as an inseparable but unconfused union of the two qualitatively different existences of Creator and creature. The crucifixion is the axle on which this 'movement' turns. It is the core of the event of the Being of God in union with what he has created as he creates it, overcoming all that threatens that created existence – the threat of non-being to created existence with all the temporal/spatial expressions of that threat, mortality and frailty, death and evil, and all the shadows of the darkness of that 'nothing-ness'. It is the crucible out of which the contingency to God and the contingency from God, whereby creation may be the creation it is, is poured, moulded and forced out in perfect harmony.

That perfect harmony of creation in relation to the Creator is declared in resurrection and ascension. There, the fulness of being of all that exists in its temporal/spatial nature is established in relation to the divine Existence.

This is not a swallowing up of the created in the divine, an absorption of the 'room' which creation has as creation in a greater 'room' of the existence of God. Rather the 'space and place' of creation is affirmed in its integrity as that which is in relation to the Creator in his 'space and place'. Its existence is verified to be genuine created existence in concord with his Existence.

By resurrection and ascension the open-ness of creation to its Creator, the way it can be understood as the creation it is, is found. Clearly, this open-ness is not self-evident from the side of creation by itself; nor is that understanding automatically, mechanically and immediately obvious. There are still the shadows on the face of its existence, for frailty and mortality characterize it.

But here again I appeal to the illustration of the single beam of light refracted into its constituent colours. The refractions are our working out in temporal/spatial experiences and circumstances that which is dynamically and 'instantly' present to God. The groaning and travailing of creation is its participation in the crucifixion.

Our *life is hid with Christ in God*[1]. We are already dead and raised with Him, as St Paul says. The refraction is our temporal/spatial working out of that 'already' which is evident only in the Place of God's Existence. The space of this creation, the totality of all its places as they are in themselves and as they exist in interaction with each other, is related to that divine Place in its Creator become one of his own creatures in the midst of that space. His 'place' as the Word made flesh gathers up all space and every place. What we call 'space' is the working out in its places of that accomplished recapitulation in the Word made flesh in his incarnation, crucifixion, resurrection and ascension as the mode of the act of God creating.

The Place of God speaks of the nature of his Existence as God. The 'place' of creation speaks of its existence as creation. Resurrection and ascension are the establishment of that 'movement' whereby the existence of creation is established in the Existence of God. But in that divine Existence, all things and all time are 'instantly' present – and they are present in Christ, the Word made flesh. Incarnation, crucifixion, resurrection and ascension are, as must be underlined, the mode of God's act of creation, all time and events being 'present' to God. When we say that the place of creation participates in the Place of God – that is that our created existence is established in God's Existence with Christ – all questions and statements concerning the presence of God – 'Where is God?'; 'God is everywhere' – become banal and superficial. In so asking and stating, we have turned the issue upside down. The question should be 'where do we participate in God?' and the answer 'Everywhere and at all times in Christ'.

This open-ness of creation to God is not – again it must be emphasised – any superficial 'Natural Theology', wherein God can be read off the face of creation. It is Christ-centred. It is a Christological statement. Only in this context can the events and circumstances of creation be seen to have their full significance and be interpreted accordingly. The movement of resurrection and ascension is the opening out of our place to that Place where Christ has gathered up all things and time in God, and firmly anchored them there. It is not a 'cosmic' journey, it is God's Existence lovingly interacting with what he creates as he creates. In our refracted time and place, Christ has his place as an historical event. But his place in the midst of the space of creation is the transfixing of all time and things to the Place of God. It is the act of creation worked out for and in the reality of our created space.

The existence of creation, its space and its places, in this Christological context, has a natural theology appropriate to it. What is not of propriety in accordance with the nature of the place of creation is that intellectual attempt to read out of creation a self-explanatory concept of infinity and eternity and identify that with God, as though God were nature writ large, or that emotional perception of God in the beauties of nature. Both these approach God by quantifying – the first by enlargement of creation, the second by selection (for it does not deal in the tragedies or the ugliness of nature).

But there can be an honest intellectual approach which sees this open-ness to God in the Word made flesh which treats the realities of this created dimension in their integrity and has due respect and regard for them. This will perceive it as a creation which in its totality is open to its Creator, and within that totality composed of levels of existence, which, in their relation one to another, correspond to that prime relation of open-ness, for lower levels of existence find their fulfilment in that above each one of them.

This multi-layered order of existences may be seen in the overlap of the various sciences which, at the boundaries of their particular levels of enquiry are open to other levels or fields of enquiry. There is an integration among all branches of knowledge – or, at least, there should be. Nothing has been more damaging to the discovery and use of the created realities than a closed, segregated way of looking at one level of existence and interpreting that out of itself. This can lead, and has led, to malevolent technology, where violence is done to the nature of a field of objects as they are wrested out of their proper context and direction of potential fulfilment. This may be observed not only environmentally, but socially and medically as well. The question 'What is man?' cannot be answered in the isolation of anthropological studies or evolutionary development, for the human being is not merely a biological or a behaviouristic episode.

In the same way, the incarnation, the resurrection or the ascension, cannot be interpreted and explained in terms of the level of human biology. Any attempt to do so can only lead to their dismissal and discarding. They certainly concern human existence, but their significance as events cannot be grasped out of that consideration alone. Under this stricture must come the tiresome search for the 'historical Jesus'.

While Jesus Christ is an historical factor, his significance as an historical factor is that he is also the Person and event of the Word made flesh. Only in terms of the Existence which gave all other things existence can he, and his significance, be understood.

This has its correspondence, again, in the sciences, where certain phenomena are not explicable on the level on which they are found, but require to be put into the context of the higher level to which they point in order to become intelligible. It is this perception of the co-ordinated levels of existence, and correspondingly co-ordinated levels of thought, which is one of Einstein's contributions to the advancement of understanding.

Equally, therefore, there can be an honest emotional 'natural theology', which is aware of the relation of all things

to God in Christ, perceives the correspondence to that relation in the awe and wonder of the created realities unfolding
in their related rationalities, and receives all this with thanksgiving for and through Christ.

The 'movement' of the ascension is not a question of something from a lower dimension rising spatially to a higher. It is
to be understood in its essence as the dynamic declaration
that the fulfilment of all created entities in their totality is to
be interpreted in the relation they have in Christ to that
Transcendent Reality in which, in him, they have their
context. Just as light is the universal constant to which, on
the created level, all temporal/spatial realities are related and
on which they depend for their particular and varied existences and identities, so, too, the context of that created
light, and therefore the existence of all things, is related to
that Uncreated Light which is God himself.

The ascension is the dynamic declaration of the recapitulation of all created realities and levels, their order, harmony
and rationality, established in the integrity of their existence
by their taking up into, and given 'place' in, the integrity of
the Creator's Triune Existence. The ascension is the open-
ness of creation's 'place' to have communion with the 'Place'
of God, the communion of creaturely existence with its
Creator's.

The essence of the ascension, what it is, is accompanied by
a sign. According to the biblical witness, this was the eleva-
tion of our Lord from earth to the heaven above, where *a
cloud received him out of their sight.*[2] The sign is spatially
given. But this spatial element is not its content. It points
appropriately in spatial dimensions to that content. We have
to distinguish (as with the incarnation accompanied by the
sign of the so-called Virgin Birth, and the resurrection by the
empty tomb) between the sign and that which is signified by
the sign. The content is not worked out by the sign. As
Irenaeus pointed out[3]:

> God giving this sign, man not working it out.

The sign is given as appropriate to our spatial existence and
to our understanding limited by that. It points beyond itself
to the Place of that Existence which gives spatial being its

created existence and its fulfilment, and to the relation of the place of creation to that Place.

This is set out in that we are told that *a cloud received him out of their sight*. 'Cloud' in biblical usage signifies that mystery of God which is beyond humanity's comprehension. It is into that mystery of God's Existence that Christ, in our fulfilled flesh and nature 'ascends'. In other words, it is a sign appropriate to the content of the ascension event, which is God making room for our created existence in the room of his Uncreated Existence.

We are also told that Christ ascends into 'heaven'. This is the second factor which we need to consider which is also raised by the ascension narrative.

The biblical witness, when it speaks of God and humanity, also employs the parallel, corresponding phrase *heaven and earth*. These, however, are not to be equated. *Earth* is the context in which humanity is placed. *Heaven* is not the context of God in which He lives and moves and has His Being, as though, like humanity related to the earth by being of the earth and limited by the earth, He is contained by heaven which determines the nature of His Being. Heaven is certainly described as God's *dwelling place*, but, clearly, this cannot be interpreted to mean that it has spatial dimensions when this usage is applied to it. There is ambiguity here.

The use of the term *heaven* in the biblical writings is two-fold. In the first place, it is regarded as part of the totality of creation. In the first verse of Genesis it is said that *In the beginning God created the heaven and the earth*. This usage is sometimes found in the plural: *the heavens and the earth*[4]. Again, the term *heaven of heavens* is found[5], suggesting that the heavens are manifold or hierarchical. This diversity, however, is included within the created order, for *heaven* or *the heavens* are the work of God's hands. He *stretches out* the heavens[6], or *bows them down*[7]. They can be *shaken*[8], made to *tremble*[9], *rent*[10], *rolled up*[11], *perish*[12] and so on.

There is a relation and a correspondence between heaven and earth. Just as there are terrestrial bodies, so there are heavenly bodies[13]; just as every knee on earth shall bow to Christ and acknowledge him as Creator and Redeemer, so there are knees in heaven which genuflect likewise to the same end [14]; just as the earth can be desolate, so too the heavens can be wrapped in the darkness of mourning[15]; just as earth can rejoice and be glad, so too heaven can[16]; and both find their fulfilment in being summed up, gathered together, in Christ, the Head of all creation[17]. This recapitulation is of heaven and of earth and of the relation between them, which consists in their complementarity in the common grounding of their creation[18].

In all such, heaven or the heavens, are in conjunction with earth, related to it and interacting upon it. In this, God is active and uses heaven or the heavens for his decrees and purposes. Heaven or the heavens, as far as the biblical witness seems to indicate in the many instances of its use of the terms, are, in spatial language, hierarchical. The terms are variously employed.

In some instances they refer to the observable heavens, the sphere of sun, moon and stars. In others they mean that which is closed to human sight, the domain of angels, archangels, and the whole heavenly host. It must be acknowledged that, depending on the particular biblical source and its outlook and background, these two treatments of the meaning of heaven or the heavens sometimes intermingle. The same sphere above is partly that of the visible creation of the sun, moon and stars, and partly the realm of the heavenly host; the 'angels of light' and the 'stars of the morning' are not always distinguishable. The heavenly host sometimes includes the heavenly bodies.

But, apart from various cosmologies which may be deduced from biblical interpretation, and of import for our purposes here, the common theme running throughout all these observations about heaven or the heavens, however, is that they are a created counterpart to earth, and form the limits of both creation and creaturely understanding.

There are two points of import here. 1. That the heavens or heaven are created; they are not 'eternal': 2. That there is a distinction, despite some confused cosmologies (for even they implicitly point to the matter) between 'heaven' as the existence of the sun, moon, stars and all the heavenly bodies, and 'heaven' as God's 'dwelling place'.

1. The Genesis narrative explicitly speaks of God creating

the heavens and the earth[19]. God has made heaven and the heaven of heavens and all their host which worships him[20]. Here we have an all-embracing reference in which all heavenly existences, those of the heaven of heavens and those of the visible heaven above, are included under the heading of that which is created. There are numerous references in such vein, but nowhere is there biblical justification for regarding the heavens, of whatever category, as 'eternal' in themselves and by themselves.

2. God, and the qualities of God, are described frequently in the biblical sources as being 'higher' than the visible heavens and even the heaven of heavens[21]. Our Lord himself has ascended above the heavens[22]. This not only refers to the heavens, but to the angelic beings who inhabit this heavenly state. These are created[23], and they are created in and by and for Christ, whether they are *thrones*, *dominions*, *principalities* or *powers* over which he has the priority and the upholding lordship[24].

The apocalyptic visions of St John in *The Revelation* all show the angelic powers and the hierarchy of heavenly beings as subservient to and worshipping God the Father and His Word and Spirit, not only as the fulfilment of their vocation, but as an example to humanity as the fulfilment of its existence.

What these two points together emphasise is that God is other than the heavens and the earth, even the heaven of heavens. And he is other in a way which, without the spatial content of the terms, 'magnifies' him 'above' them. He is other than, and therefore distinct from, them. It is not heaven which creates the earth, nor is it the angels. It is God who creates the heavens and the heaven of heavens and the earth. The *all things* of Ephesians I:10 and Colossians I:20 mean literally that – all things which are not God.

Heaven is not to be thought of as a dimension which God happens to inhabit – an 'eternity' or an 'infinity' for which his being and nature is adapted. If it is said that he inhabits the heavens, it is also said that the heavens cannot contain him.

What we are left with is the assertion that God exists as God uniquely. There is no other form of existence, or sphere for existence, which is commensurable. It is difficult to think about this, for the prevailing tendency of our thoughts is to position God and put him in context. This is because we inevitably lapse into a 'container' way of thinking about the nature of things, God included, or a way of thinking in which the need not to forsake measurability for fear of not grasping, dominates. We find it singularly difficult to empty our concepts of spatial and temporal content when applying them to God. Our images of God have to be applied 'imagelessly', that is, without the cloying spatial and temporal content they have when applied to the created realities.

It is this constant desire to hold on to some form of measure – even if it is beyond our mathematical ability to complete the sum of what we are thinking about, and call it 'infinity' or 'eternity', so that our minds have what we think to be rational control – which causes the difficulty in thinking about God. We have to learn to think in a way which corresponds, as far as is humanly possible, to the rationality of God, to that which he is as he exists as God. This is not the same as the rationality we employ in thinking about created things in general. Even within that generality of the created order, we have to learn to think about things not in terms of some general rationality, but in accordance to what they are in themselves.

For example, there is every difference in the world between the mode of thought required to analyse, understand, describe and fittingly work on, an inanimate piece of wood, and an organism such as the human eye. Carpenters are not eye surgeons, nor do eye surgeons use the same tools of trade as carpenters. An eye surgeon may also work with wood as a hobby, but he must surely switch his mode of rationality and operation from the pursuit of his hobby to the exercise of his vocation if he wishes to avoid dire results to his patient.

We are faced with having to think about existences which are different from each other in the created dimension. This is the essence of that κατὰ φύσιν, that *according to nature* thinking of which we spoke earlier. In this, we think out of a centre in the reality which confronts us.

But, as has been underlined already, we cannot rise up and

burst the bounds of created limitations and corresponding rationality, to find God. We are very much forced back to the historical event anchored at the heart of creation of the Word made flesh, where and when God comes to us on his own terms. It is there that 'heaven is bent down to earth and earth bent up to heaven', to use the language of the old theologians.

It is here that the ascension of Christ 'into heaven' is of paramount importance, and we have to think out of this event concerning the Person of Christ as God and man. For, as we have emphasised throughout, this is God confronting us, on his own terms in the midst of our realities, having taken the limitations of the created reality to himself in confronting man as this man Jesus.

The Nicene-Constantinopolitan Creed affirms this ascension of Jesus *into heaven*. But first, as the distillation of the whole biblical witness, it speaks of heaven and earth as a created, two-fold dimension, bringing both into relation with the Triune God in its assertion that *God the Father Almighty* is the *Maker of heaven and earth, and of all things visible and invisible*; that Jesus Christ as *God of God, Light of Light*, is the One *by whom all things were made*; and that the Holy Spirit, with the Father and the Son is *worshipped and glorified*.

Here the Creed has taken a developed view of those elements wherein heaven is more cosmologically expressed in the Biblical witness in both Old and New Testaments.

Heaven is clearly now that invisible 'realm' of creation, distinguished from all that is visible, which visibility includes the cosmological heavens even if these, in their farthest reaches, are beyond the perception of humanity. This, of course, is an element also found in the biblical witness, but not necessarily always distinguishable from the 'sphere' of sun, moon and stars.

The Creed brings out that to which the biblical witness pointed; namely that there is a heaven which is invisible and of which the visible heavens are the sign in their 'aboveness' to the earth, in their immensity over the more humble things of earth, and in their mystery which overwhelms earthly minds. These heavens, the 'superior' part of the two-fold spatial and temporal creation, point to that heaven of God. They are but the created sign of that which is qualitatively different from them, though it too, as the heaven of God, is distinct from God and the work of his hands.

It is this qualitative distinction which has to be acknowledged. That is, that the heaven of which the Creed speaks is not, even if created, of the same nature of existence as the heavens above the earth. These latter may be observed; the former is veiled from the processes of human sight and the competence of human understanding because of its distinction from the temporal/spatial creation. It is as preposterous to build an intellectual Tower of Babel whose top tries to reach heaven, as it is to build a physical one. It is inaccessible to us.

The crux of the matter is that we cannot think of heaven as though it were a dimension which exists of itself and within which there are heavenly beings engaged on some sort of heavenly activity. We can only think of the existence and activity of God. When it is said that heaven is God's *habitation*[25], or, more commonly, his *throne*[26], this is not a static concept, much less of a spatial nature. It refers to the rule of God, his exercise of his dominion over all things.

Corresponding to this on the temporal/spatial dimension, we have the glimmering of the same sort of usage in the monarch's throne, the professorial chair, the episcopal cathedra. All these in their respective ways point essentially to the authority, wisdom and pastoral guardianship of those whose possessions they are. They do not limit or contain the occupants, but point to the office and exercise of vocation. As tangible signs they are nothing apart from that which they signify.

Heaven is the result of the presence and the activity of God. It is other than God, but related to his presence and activity in a way utterly distinct from the relation of the temporal/spatial creation to him. It is that mode of creation which is appropriate to its 'immediacy' to God. Yet even this heaven of God is not without the heavens and the earth, the totality of the created universe, for it has a relation with them.

The ascension of Christ into heaven is the ascension to the

'right hand' of God. Again, it will not do to convey and project the material content of such terminology, what it normally means when applied to the temporal/spatial realities, even symbolically. The 'right hand' refers to the fact that Christ exercises that dominion of God as one with the Father and the Spirit. The Father, at the ascension, sets him[27]

> at his own right hand in the heavenly places.
> far above all principality, and power, and might, and dominion, and every name that is named, not only in this world, but also in that which is to come.

But this is done on the basis that Christ has been raised from the dead, that the universal creation is transformed in him, the recapitulation of all that is created. The ascension means that heaven is typified by what Christ has done on earth, and, in one sense, earth with its heavens above it as the totality of the temporal/spatial creation, determines the nature of heaven. Indeed, again in one sense, it takes precedence, for we are expressly exhorted to take note of the fact that the Word[28]

> took not on him the nature of angels, but he took on him the seed of Abraham.

That is to say, the angelic existences were by-passed in favour of humanity. The angels, according to the writer of the *Epistle to the Hebrews*[29], are to be regarded as ministering spirits to humanity on the basis of this work of the incarnate Word. The 'higher' serves the 'lower' because the Creator has declared that humanity and the temporal/spatial realities, are in an even closer relation to him than are the angelic host.

It is in a consideration of this 'service' by the angels that we find a heightening of what we may legitimately say about heaven without overstretching ourselves. Heaven is the doing of the will of God. *Thy will be done in earth, as it is in heaven.* The biblical narratives, throughout the Old and New Testament, depict angels (of whose nature very little is said, their appearances to the human recipients of their visitations, differing) as those bearing witness to the glory, the majesty of God and the corresponding acts of God towards creation.

In some instances, for example the appearances in the Abraham saga in *Genesis*, the angelic presences are more or less manifestations of God himself. They do not speak of themselves; they bear no witness as to their existences; their sole function is to witness to God and proclaim his activity. They are servants of God, doing his bidding. That there is a pleroma of angelic beings in the biblical narratives merely emphasises the variety and richness of the works of God towards creation. The variety is in their service, not in their supposed status. The titles variously given to 'orders' within the heavenly host are descriptions of that varied service and function, rather than a catalogue of static hierarchies within the angelic ranks.

But all these angelic services are directed to the fulfilment of the covenant with Israel in the Word made flesh and to the witnessing of that event.

> No man has ascended up to heaven, but he that came down from heaven, even the Son of man which is in heaven[30].

Here, if we will have it, is the substance of the sign of Jacob's Ladder, that the biblical insistence through the deployment of angels, that there is a constant concourse, conversation and companying of this heaven with the heavens and the earth, is gathered together and is found in the 'descent' of the Word made flesh and in his 'ascent'. Here, in this Jesus, is *none other but the house of God, and the gate of heaven*[31]. The Word made flesh is God's 'place' within humanity's 'place'. His ascension is the taking of humanity's 'place' into God's 'place'. Apart from this 'descent' and 'ascent', the angels and their activities have no significance. They serve it as *ministering spirits*, as the witnesses to the being and acts of God.

Karl Barth in his comprehensive discussion about the Kingdom of Heaven in *Church Dogmatics, III:3*, pp. 418ff, notes the emphasis on this service of the angelic host in the biblical narratives. It is here, he points out, that so many of the Fathers and the Mediaeval thinkers who entered the field of speculation about angels went astray. Angels cannot be known apart from this service, from their functions. It is their raison d'être. We have criticized Pseudo-Dionysius already on this sort of matter, and here Barth makes the assertion[32], that the Pseudo-Areopagite's foray into the matter of analysing the ranks of angels from the basis of biblical references

> reached the very limit of arbitrariness and futility.

Barth continues:

> If there is order in heaven, it is not the order of rank, but of function and service.

He does see in Pseudo-Dionysius sufficient description and treatment of the angelic beings dynamically, for in these writings the author does stress to some extent the activity of the heavenly host in all its variety. This, says Barth, gives us cause not to exclude the possibility that, for all his errors of judgment and approach to the matter, Pseudo-Dionysius may be regarded as

> a man who unfortunately spoke of an order of rank but perhaps had in mind an order of service.

What begins to unfold from all this is the removal of all static concepts of heaven. Heaven's 'place' is not of this genre; it is not observable or measurable. Nor is it explicable in the limited language with its necessarily spatial overtones and static undertones, which we have at our disposal. The best we can say is that it is 'place' in the sense of the result of the activity of God's rule and majesty and grace. If it is 'peopled' with angelic existences, they serve that dominion, and that service too is of the essence of heaven.

It is not because there is heaven that there is a God who happens to inhabit such a domain. It is because there is such a God as the God who creates in that rule and majesty and grace, which is his overflowing love in creating that which is other than himself, that there is a heaven. This heaven is integral to that creative love. It is a result of it.

Equally, it is not a heaven in isolation from the rest of creation, that is, this dimension which we know, these heavens and this earth of ours. For central to heaven is the figure of our Lord, the Word made flesh, to whom all authority in heaven and earth has been given. In himself, as the one by whom all things are made, for whom they were made, and in whom they consist – and this includes heaven – all is recapitulate, summed up, and presented to God in their fulfilment.

All time and things are dynamically present to God in this fulfilment of them in Christ, of which fulfilment the temporal/spatial realities of which we are a part and which characterise how we live and move and have our being, are, through Christ, pointers.

The new heavens and the new earth, which are seen as the disclosure of the work of Christ, the transformation of all creation at the fulfilment of this refracted time and space of ours, are already a fact in him. They are there in that heaven of God with Christ as the characteristic form of it. Indeed, Karl Rahner can write[33] that the resurrection created 'heaven', and that the resurrection with the ascension is not merely an entry into an already existing heaven – for the ascension is the ascension of the resurrected body of Christ, the flesh and nature of human reality, and with it all created reality, transformed in its fulfilment of its union with God, whereby its integrity is declared and established, and characterizing heaven.

The resurrection appearances, as recounted in the Gospels, all point to the created reality of Christ's risen humanity, the 'place' of human being fulfilled in its union with the 'place' of God, as not bound and constricted by time and space, which are the hallmarks of refracted human being and the refracted dimension in which we live, move and have our being. They point to what the fulfilment of that refraction is in Christ, who rises as the recapitulation of it all. This is why the risen Christ is beyond the constrictions of space and time, yet is there in their midst, affirming what they really are in fulfilment.

The juxtaposition of the Johannine writer's observation

> it doth not yet appear what we shall be: but we know that, when he shall appear, we shall be like him; for we shall see him as he is

with St Paul's emphasis in *Colossians* that we are already dead with Christ and raised with him, and that our life is hid with Christ in God, surely lets us perceive that what will be seen, on that day which will be the fulfilment of creation, when this refracted time and space will be rolled up as a garment and seen in its totality, is 'already' a fact and an event from the side of God. Our 'place' is there with Christ in God. That, it is my thesis, is the act of creation through incarnation, and we live out, as the sort of beings we are, that fact and event refracted as space and time. That is how we come to the integrity of what we really are 'already' in Christ, which process of coming befits the nature of that which is created.

That this fulfilment of creation is a dynamic present from the side of God, and that this fulfilment is 'instantaneous' in the act of creation through incarnation, again from the side of God, characterises God's heaven. This heaven is that which is other than God in which all creation rejoices in its fulfilment and all creation gives glory and thanksgiving and praise to him.

10

Angelology and Cosmology

THIS 'instantaneity' of creation, and the 'place' of angelic beings as existences of pure light as over against our existences of refracted light while yet being integrally related to them in the totality of all creation, is brought out by Robert Grosseteste in several of his works. In his *Hexaemeron* he writes of the role of angels in God's act of creation.

In the *Hexaemeron*, the exemplarity of angels as created spiritual light, pure intelligences, contemplating and adoring and thus in closest communion with that uncreated Light which God is, is set out. They have their function as ministers of that first of God's creative acts, the calling forth of created light in its creaturely correspondence to God's uncreated Light. They are reflections of that first light, intellectual beings of sheer enlightenment.

This, for Grosseteste, is their raison d'être and service. They are ministers of light to all creation. Light pervades all creation, heavenly and earthly; it is the unifying factor of all creation, and the very epitome of all being which is contingent to and from God. They are created in and with that light. But as such, they have not only a function towards creation; they look Godwards as well. They exemplify, in its purest form, the rationality and enlightenment of creation. The angels are not emanations from God; nor are they co-creators with him. They are the purest form of creation, related as they are to that light which is, according to Grosseteste in his *De Luce*, the first corporeal form, the purest and swiftest energy.

Here I must expand on Grosseteste's thesis regarding angels, and therefore the nature of heaven. To do so, I revert to much of what I said about his angelology in *The Anachronism of Time*. But first it is as well to draw attention to Karl Barth's strictures in the matter of speaking or writing about angels[1].

He cautions us that regarding angels there has always been a great deal of theological caprice,

> of valueless, grotesque and even absurd speculation, and also of no less doubtful scepticism.

He says that those who say too much and those who deny too much with regard to angels lack a sense of humour. Whenever Barth mentions a sense of humour, he puts the practice of theology in its right perspective. No matter how eminent a theologian one or another may be, both are but men, and they must have the gift of being able to laugh at themselves as just human beings thinking that they can tackle the gargantuan task of the profound issues which theology lays upon them. In other words, they must not take themselves too seriously, otherwise they will think too highly of themselves, elevating opinions into dogmas and deeming their all too fallible words as something approaching, if not on par with, the Word of God.

The early church knew, in some quarters at any rate, that such a recognition of human limitations in the subject was necessary. Origen[2], even Origen, could say that although the church proclaimed the existence of angels, there is no sure knowledge of them. Gregory of Nazianzus[3] likewise later noted the difficulty of finding any terminology to speak about angels. For the main part, the biblical instances of angelic visitations show that they come, they go and they do not tarry long enough for attention to be fixed on them. Their import is their message. They are self-effacing; their being is totally of that of service to God and humanity. They are, as Barth remarks[4]

> essentially marginal figures. This is their glory. It is in their subordination to the great events acted out between God and man that they are that praeclarum et nobile specimen of the creaturely world.

They are attendants on the Lordship of the King of Heaven and of the heavens and of the earth, as it is expressed in His acts and works and words towards and in creation. As such, they can only be described in terms of biblical saga and legend. But this does not detract from their reality. Because we have no language appropriate to their existences, that

most certainly does not mean that they do not exist. And if
the language of biblical legend and saga is used of them –

> this does not mean that we are in the sphere of Red Riding
> Hood and her grandmother and the wolf, or the stork which
> leaves babies, or the March Hare and Father Christmas; in a
> sphere in which the biblical authors gave free rein to their
> poetic imagination, and in which we can give ourselves up
> with abandon to the same indulgence. This is not the case. For
> there can be meaningful as well as meaningless imagination,
> and disciplined as well as undisciplined poetry – this is the
> difference between good saga and bad. Both imagination and
> poetry can be ordered by orientation on the subject and its
> inner order ... Even in relation to the angels we are not left
> without any thoughts at all, or in the sphere of dreams or day-
> dreams, but we are summoned to think with true theological
> knowledge in which it will be shown that no indolence is
> possible in this sphere, that divinatory thinking and speech
> are indispensable, but that we are not allowed to think and
> speak anything and everything, that the angels and the March
> Hare are two different things, that in relation to angels we are
> commanded to think and say something very definite – vera,
> certa and utilia ...[5]

Robert Grosseteste, standing out in the midst of so much of
the speculation of the Middle Ages, treats the subject of
angels in a manner which fulfils what Barth has observed. In
general, he treats angels in the context of light – the Light
which God is and the light of creation corresponding to that
Uncreated Light.

Angelology for Grosseteste is a secondary feature of little
independent import, save where the subject of angels is used
as a clarification of the question of the place of light and
understanding in creation.

There is a juxtaposition of angels, light, the nature of
creation and knowledge. His angelology is set out for the
most part in his little treatise *De Intelligentiis*, the second
part of a long letter addressed to Master Adam Rufus who
had posed questions to him. This deals with angels as
messengers and ministers of God, and not their significance
for Grosseteste's mind in relation to creation and light. But
even here, using a quotation from Augustine[6], he warns
against projecting material thoughts into things spiritual,

conceiving such in 'sensuous' images. Angels are not creatures as we are.

One of his *Charges to the Clergy*[7] sets out the angels' relationship to God as determinative of their status and function.
Here, they are regarded as pure, intellectual substances,
whose singular function of intelligence is fixed solely on the
contemplation of the Trinity. The Word is their mirror and
their book in Whom they see eternity and life, and the
majesty, might, wisdom and grace of God. All that they are
in their existence as they who so contemplate, adore and act,
is a singular and simple expression of spiritual light, such as
humanity should long for but, though incapable of achieving
it, yet must seek it even within our limitations and weakness.

The exemplarity of angels as created spiritual light
contemplating and adoring and thus sharing in uncreated
Light, is best set out in the *Hexaemeron*. Here[8] Grossetese
claims that angels are not excluded from the creation narrative. In the very creation of light their creation is contained.
They are reflections of the first light, for they are pure intelligences, intellectual beings of sheer enlightenment. As such,
they call humanity to an awareness of the nature of light
created and Light Uncreated. Light is the purest form of
matter. In the symbolism of Genesis, both the creation of
angels and the ground and form of all created things is light
itself. Light is inextricably woven to the concept of order;
indeed, light is order and order is light. Light is seen in the
first instance as that which is Uncreated Light, the order
which God eternally is in Himself as Father, Son bound in the
bond of eternal Love, the Holy Spirit. This uncreated Light is
reflected in the created light, which is the form and the quality most approximate to that which God is as uncreated
Light. This created light manifests itself throughout the
orders of angels, in their particular state, and then into the
spatial/temporal existence of all the created orders of the
heavens and the earth. It is the unifying factor of all creation,
heavenly and earthly, spiritual and material, and as that
factor, that which is supremely contingent to and from the
uncreated Light of God Himself.

In positing a particular angelology in which angels, created
with the creation of light as the first form of all creation, are

regarded as transcending this gulf in their very being, and by insisting generally on a two-fold noetic and ontic role of light as the ground of all created being in form and matter, both spiritual and material, Grosseteste removes himself from all the then prevailing dichotomies in mediaeval thought between these categories. As that which pervades and characterises all creation, heavenly and earthly, light transcends any dualistic gulf, and is both the unifying factor of all creation and the principium of contingency to and from God. It binds the quality of heaven to the quality of the temporal/spatial heavens and earth.

By *spiritual* Grosseteste means above all *intellectual* or *intelligent being* – intellectual and intelligent, referring not to cleverness, but to that which is in such a relation to God that its understanding and existence is formed by the sheer bond of its contingency to, and the nearness of its obedient contingency from, Him. That is why though humanity is of flesh and blood it nevertheless within the limits of this condition is to realize that it is 'spiritual' in this sense. It is bound to heaven by light, and thus space is related to that non-spatial and non-temporal heaven by light.

His was a unitary, as opposed to the prevailing dualistic, way of thinking. And this way of thinking is based on the status and role of light in its relation to uncreated Light. This is clear from his observation on the senses, which he divides into external and internal. Of the external, sight is the prime sense, and by nature, different from the other four, because light is both the object which gives the ability to see, and that which enlightens what is seen.

There is an order and a gradation of the senses, for they are linked to an order and gradation of the things for which they were created. Hearing, smell, taste and touch, all are graded according to the heaviness or thickness of the elements concerned. Hearing comes from the higher, finer air; smell from the thicker, lower air; taste from water activity; touch from material itself. But all these are bonded together in their respective places in this descending order, by light in its descent to the gross elements in which its activity is weaker the lower the element, but nevertheless active.

This distribution of matter in more and more solid quantity, is explained, as we have seen, in *De Luce*. At creation, light, created as a simple point, expands infinitely (in our calculation). This expansion spreads matter spherically, equally in every direction, such is the movement of light, from that simple point of no dimension. Expanding by sphere upon sphere (nine heavenly and four lower in all, according to Grosseteste, following the then generally accepted Patristic observances) each of the nine spheres is qualified by the action of *lux* propagating *lumen*, light begetting light, and light begotten by light – a derivative process. But because it is derivative, the process is characterised by increasing weakness, which results in increasing density and loss of purity owing to the diminishing power of lumen from sphere to sphere. Light is simpler and purer in the higher and heavenly spheres, more diverse and corporeal in the lower. But light binds heaven and the heavens and the earth. For it is in its full purity and simplicity in heaven, but refracted in all else.

The unity of all created things in their respective places, and therefore of all space, is contained in that first light. All things, so concluded, are present in that initial simple singularity of light, the first created form and corporeity itself. It is the unity of all things in their diversity, their order and their harmony, and the totality of their existence. It is recapitulation in reverse – all things first contained in the simple point of light at its creation, and then spread into their places according to their quality and nature determined by the quality, nature and activity of light.

It is to be noted, however, that for Grosseteste, this hierarchy is no static concept. It is a matter of the dynamism of light and its results. Thus light is the *principium unitatis* of all things, bestowing rationality and order, pervading and adorning the confronting object and the knowing subject, giving order and intelligibility externally and internally. In *De Luce*, Grosseteste describes light as *species et perfetio corporum omnium* – the glory and perfection of all embodied things.

But light is indivisible – both spatially and temporally. Here we must concern ourselves with the nature of created light at creation itself, and what Grosseteste's angelology has to add in the understanding of this.

We occupy ourselves here with his insistence on harmony and order in the dynamic and active hierarchical placement of angelic beings. This is a far cry from Pseudo-Dionysius's static concept of celestial hierarchy.

What is pertinent and of import is the conjunction of angels and the 'days' of creation as recounted in Genesis. The angels enjoy undiminishing contemplation and uninterrupted clarity of the vision of God. It is this privileged sight which gives them their place in the creative act of God.

The danger exhibited in the works of some mediaeval writers on the subject is that the angels are described in terms of being mediators, and, in some instances agents, in the work of creation. This may well be the influence of those Arabic commentators on cosmology – Averroës (Ibn Rushd), Avicebrol (Solomon Ibn Gebirol) and Avicenna (Ibn Sina) – to whom the west, in the 12th and 13th centuries, looked for their valued commentaries on the classical Greek philosophers. While Grosseteste had recourse to these, and his dependence on them is clear, he would have none of this.

Although angels have pre-eminence of being, being pure spirit, they are created beings, whatever pre-eminence in the orders of creation they enjoy. And they are created not to be co-creators with God. There is a decisive qualitative difference between Creator and created. There is no blurring of the edges by introducing emanations from God in a descending scale to present, in the fashion of dualistic thought, a protection for God against being tainted with having anything to do with matter.

Rather, as has been stressed above, the angels are exemplary in their contemplation of God and the acts of God. They are ideals whose state it is impossible for humanity to achieve but towards such like it nevertheless must seek to strive within its grosser limitations.

It is their relation to light which forms the key to unlock the answer to their import vis-a-vis God and the rest of creation. Indeed much of what may be said of light may be said of the angelic state and function. I suspect that Grosseteste unwittingly relates them to time, for they are concerned with the movement and action of light, as well as so closely participating in its nature and quality.

This train of thought is set out in his *De Cessatione Legalium*, and in the *Commentary on the Posterior Analytics*, but most profoundly in the *Hexaemeron*. It is in the last that the role of angels in the creative act of God is stressed. In *De Cessatione Legalium*, Grosseteste clearly asserts the simultaneity of all creation on the basis of the text of Ecclesiasticus, chapter 18, verse 1:

Qui vivit in aeternum creavit omnia simul.

He who lives eternally created all things simultaneously

He develops this in the *Hexaemeron*, questioning why Augustine is less decisive in the matter than Jerome and Basil who state the simultaneity of all creation clearly[9]. He certainly uses Augustine's work[10] as part basis for his development of the simultaneity of creation and the place of angels in this act of God. However, the question must be asked if Grosseteste is not also and more so, dependent on John Philoponus, the 6th century Alexandrian grammarian. He neither makes mention of the name nor acknowledges any source for his statements, but the parallelism of thought is remarkable. The particular point of remark is that Grosseteste looks, certainly as Augustine did, on the relation between angels and days in the Genesis narrative. But while Augustine[11] identifies the angels with the days of creation (days being light and angels light also) Grosseteste sees this relation in a far more involved and intriguing way in terms of the simultaneity of creation.

Augustine describes the days of creation as the cognition of the orders of creation within the angelic mind. As pure intelligences, the angels perceive the development of creation as unfolding in sequence, though the cycle of each day and the events therein are, in temporal terms, simultaneous. The first day consists of the angel's knowledge of itself, the second of the firmament, and then on through the rest of the created orders including the creation of humanity on the sixth day. The 'days' are characterised not by time, in our sense, but by the threefold process of cognition set out in terms of the brightest light (mid-day), the dimmest light (evening) and the dawning light (morning). The brightest light is the angelic perception of the particular order of creation seen in the decree of the eternal Word; the dimmest light the cognition of that order realized and made by the Word; and the dawning light the perception of the relation of the particular order to the Word by Whom it was created, that is, its contingency to and from the Word.

The problem left by Augustine is typified by his statement[12] that

> Time does not exist without some movement and transition … Then assuredly the world was made not in time, but simultaneously with time. For that which is made in time is made both after and before some time – after that which is past, before that which is future. But none could then be past, for there was no creature by whose movement its duration could be measured. But simultaneously with time the world was made, if in the world's creation change and motion were created as seems evident from the order of the first six or seven days.

There is an unresolved ambiguity here, caused by the particular use of change and motion in conjunction with *time*, so that although the simultaneity of creation is stressed, nevertheless the creation is seen as a successive temporal unfolding of moments simultaneous in each day only. While Grosseteste follows this, he deals more determinedly and firmly with what is left untied together untidily by Augustine, namely the question of the simultaneity of the whole process of creation, the apparent sequence of 'days' and what is meant by *change* and *motion* in the act of creation. This he does by his exposition of the angelic cognition of creation and its orders[13]. Not only in the sequence of each 'day', but in the totality of the 'days' of creation is there simultaneity. Moreover, and most importantly, angels, for Grosseteste, transcend space and time, or rather, bear a superior relation to all space and time. This development runs clearly throughout those passages dealing with angelology in the *Hexaemeron*. This relation can only be if all space and time is recapitulate in that Primordial Point of light, that Singularity of creation. Change and motion are in relation to recapitulative space and time.

The first 'day' creation of light is not only of light itself but of being-in-light and being-of-light – the creation of the angelic existence. The cycle of brightness, dimmer light and dawn light consists of the angel's cognition of its being in the Divine mind and decree, the knowledge of itself which (it being lesser than the Divine) means that this dimmer light corresponds to the awareness of the angel in realizing its difference from and dependence on God – its contingency to and from God in His creative love and grace – and finally the dawn light of its contemplation of its being and role in relation to the Triune existence of the eternal Creator. So too, on the second day, the creation of the firmament, the angelic cognition perceives it in the Divine mind, as actualized and in its relation to the Creator.

The development of Grosseteste from Augustine is that the whole creation process is simultaneous. The days are cyclical cognitions embracing the fulness of the act of creation, from the Divine decree through the actualisation of the decree to the recognition of the relation of the finished work in its contingent relation to God. He describes this cyclical process of 'days' in the angelic intelligence[14].

> *Item vespere et mane aliter intelliguntur. Prima namque lux, ut dictum est, secundum Augustinum est angelica natura ad Deum conversa, et conversione que ad Deum est deiformis effecta. In qua deiformitate ipsa est quasi lux et dies, post tenebras negacionis existencie sue et post tenebras privacionis in se naturaliter precedentis hanc lucem sue deiformitatis, que erant quasi tenebre super faciem abyssi. In hac vero luce et die cognovit Creatorem, et se ipsam in racione sua creatrice in mente divina. Huius itaque prime diei vespera est, post lucum dicte cognicionis, velud obscurior cognicio sue proprie nature in se, qua cognoscit quod ipsa non est hoc quod Deus. Cum vero, post hanc obscuriorem cognicionem sui in se, refert se ad laudandam ipsam lucem que Deus est, cuius contemplacione formatur, et percipit in ipsa luce firmamentum creandum, fit mane, finiens velud primum diem naturalem et velud inchoans secundum diem.*

Likewise 'the evening and the morning' are interpreted differently. For the first light, as we are told, is, according to Augustine, the angelic nature turned towards God, and by this turning which is towards God, it is made deiform. In this God-like form it is in itself like light and day, after the darkness of the negation of its own existence and after the darkness of privation in itself, coming naturally before this light of its God-like form, which was like the darkness on the face of the deep. Indeed in this light and day it recognized the Creator, and recognized its own reason for creation in the divine mind. And so of this first day there is an evening, after the light of the aforesaid recognition, like a darker recognition of its own nature in itself, by which it recognizes that it is not in itself that which God (is). When indeed after this darker recognition of itself in itself, it returns to prising the light which God is, by the contemplation of whom it is formed and it perceives in the light itself the creation of the firmament, (as though) it were morning, as though finishing the first natural day and as though beginning the second day.

Grosseteste's thought concerning the cyclical nature of the angel's contemplation can be summarized thus: When God says *Let there be, fiat*, the angel perceives the reason for that particular creation lodged in the eternal Word; *and so it was made, et sic est factum*, refers to the cognizance of that creation impressed on the angelic intelligence; the statement *it was so* (here *quod fecit deus*) points to the affirmation of the angel of the actuality of that creation in its tangible being. But, as there can be no intrusion of temporal values into the eternity of God, there is no time lapse between the decree, the deed and the accomplishment. The will and the act and the deed are 'instantaneous'. And this is for all the 'days' of creation; the six are but qualitative distinctions instantly accomplished.

The simultaneous cyclical cognitions, graded by light, in the angelic mind concerning all the simultaneous 'days' of creation, are accomplished in a twinkling. He illustrates this[15] by pointing out that the sun's light going through a transparent material illuminates all of it simultaneously, but those parts nearer the light more clearly.

> ... *quemadmodum solis splendor subito pertransit et simul tempore illustrat loca soli viciniora et remociora cum tamen prius natura illustret loca proximiora.*

> ... just as for instance the brightness of the sun passes through suddenly and lights up the places closer to and the parts more distant from the sun simultaneously, although however nature lights the nearest places most clearly.

What this illustration does is to show that the demarcation

into 'days' in the Genesis narrative, is not regarded by Grosseteste as a temporal division, but a division of quality determined by light. This corresponds to the statements about noonday, evening and morning light; they refer respectively to the quality perceived by the angelic mind – first the splendour of uncreated Light, God Himself, then the angel's lesser created being in itself, and last the wonder of that being in the contingent relation of grace and love to its Creator.

In same way, all the 'days' are as one, diversified only by the quality of what is perceived – on the first the pure light and angelic being, on the second the firmament, and so on until the sixth day. But the cycle of the second day is the same cycle as the first. It is differentiated not by time but by the perception of the particular order of creation concerned. And so with all the days. All the orders of creation are simultaneously perceived at the beginning – at that first act of creation, the bringing into existence of light in a twinkling, and contained within it. But what is to be noted here is the fact that the created existences are regarded as 'simultaneous', for their allotted 'times' or 'days' of creation are simultaneous. They are 'simultaneously present' in their totality.

It is the business of the angelic creation to bring creation's praise throughout the orders of creation in their diversity, before the throne of the Creator. In this respect we may see a parallel between the angels as creatures of the first light, and therefore supremely rational beings, and humanity, as the last and crown of God's creation, which with its rational mind also praises God itself for its own being and appointment and also on behalf of all else over which, in the corporeal world, it has been given dominion and responsibility. At the 'beginning' and 'end' of creation, we have the creation of rational beings, the one heavenly, the other earthly, encompassing the work of God.

It is necessary to point out that while some of the statements employed by Grosseteste would seem to suggest that he had either fallen into a general tendency or gnosticism with regard to creation, or that he was claiming the employment of particular intermediaries by God in the work of creation, he expressly repudiates such views in the

Hexaemeron. He denounces the views of Plato regarding a Demiurge who employed demigods to create matter, keeping the creation of things spiritual to himself; the 'Jewish fable' that God conversed with the angels in making man (hence 'in our image' was interpreted as that of God and the angels); and those attitudes which may well be those of the Arabic commentators following a Neo-Platonic emphasis rather like Plato himself. Grosseteste is clear, and expresses himself in no uncertain terms on the matter that the eternal Word is the eternal Son, God of God, by Whom alone the Father made all things in the bond of the Spirit – that creation is solely the work of the Triune God. The following[16] is typical of Grosseteste's linking of the all-sufficient Trinity and the work of creation:

> *Dixit itaque Deus, hoc est: Verbum sibi coeternum genuit. Diccio enim Verbi est generacio, et cum alius si qui gignit et alius qui gignitur, habes hic duas persona, Patris videlicet et Filii, pateneter expressas; et in superioribus expressus fuit Dei spiritus. Unde iam tota Trinitas expressa est; bis videlicet Pater et Filius: semel cum dictum est supra In principio fecit Deus, et iterum cum dictum est nunc Dixit Deus; et semel Spiritus Sanctus, cum dictum est: Spiritus Domini ferebatur super aquas.*

'And so God said': that is to say, He begat the Word co-eternal with Himself. For the saying of the Word is its begetting, and when one begets and another is begotten, you have here two persons, those of the Father and the Son, made manifest plainly; and the Spirit of God was made manifest earlier (in the text). From whence is the Holy Trinity now made manifest; the Father and the Son twice – once when it was said above 'In the beginning God created', and again when it is now said 'God said'; and the Holy Spirit once, when it was said 'The Spirit of the Lord was borne upon the waters'.

The Trinity is all sufficient and acts solely in that sufficiency. The role of the angels is not that of active mediators in the work of creation; they are ministers and servants, διάκονι, whose function is to understand the creative intent of the Triune God for all creation in its respective orders (including themselves) and to gather up all adoration, praise and thanksgiving for the wonders they behold. They are witnesses to the love and grace and order of the Trinity in creating immediately in the first twinkling of light all that is. In this way, light, illumination, grace and love and order are beheld and gathered up in the one instant angelic proclamation of creation before God.

This means that not only all time, which to us is divided into a past, a present and a future, is there in all its fulness and completion for God in that indescribable instant of His creation of light, but also all space exists in its fulness, being the sum total of all created existences in their 'place', that is, the nature of their existence as each is in itself and the relation of each to the rest.

The *beginning* now also refers to the *completeness* – that is to the end or the fulfilment. It is all contained in that first light. Here, of course, we are back in the realm of Christological debate concerning the Word as that light referred to in St John's Gospel, and to His work, in Irenaean terms, of *joining the end to the beginning*.

It may be said that angels are perceived, again in Irenaean terms, as the heralds of the Immeasurable confronting the measurable, the Invisible grasping the visible, the 'Place' of God taking to itself the 'place' of creation. They are creatures of pure light from 'where' the fulfilment of all creation lies in its full communion with Christ in the life of the Triune God, coming out of that fulness, the 'new heavens and the new earth', in harmony with the heaven of God, to witness to the diversity and divisions of our spatial and temporal existence that this is what is 'already' is in truth, and attendants to that act of God in Christ whereby the end of all creation is joined to the beginning in instant completion and perfection. Into our refracted and divided world they came and they come, calling it in its time and space, its whole existence, to its significance in Christ. Perhaps all the biblical references to the angels as guardians of individuals and as 'princes' of the peoples, should be seen in this light.

Heaven is the invisible and inaccessible background only seen and entered in Christ, of which these creatures of pure light are the attendants and servants, of the whole world-existence and world-history in its fulfilment. It is the 'place' of the fulfilment of all creation, 'where' every order in its created integrity and in its unity and fulfilment in the Word –

angels, humanity and all creation in harmony – finds its full
purpose in glorifying God and enjoying him in communion
with him.

Epilogue

PREACHERS in the Middle Ages frequently were advised to expound biblical texts by taking each word *cum grano salis*. That is to say, they were to be studiously careful in their treatment of words, each word being weighed against a grain of salt. Many a text has been preached and the sermon foundered upon the failure to give due place to even the smallest word. As Lancelot Andrewes warned in his exposition of James I:22[1] – *Be ye doers of the word and not hearers only, deceiving your own selves* – the failure to perceive the importance of small words can lead to totally wrong surmises. In this text, the word *only* has more place than its surface insignificance would suggest. For to omit it is to misinterpret St James as advising that we do not listen but only act, whereas

> We need to walk warily ... Saint James, by opening our hands to doe, hath no meaning to shut our eares, to heare.

We need to hear in order to act correctly, but also, we need to act and not just hear, thinking that our duty is finished with the hearing of the word. Such is the weight of the little word *only* in its context.

So it is with the words *time* and *space*. On the one hand, they are easily said, often used and rarely pondered. Our common usage betrays our indifference to what these words profoundly are, and our unthinking. I have suggested that there is a distinction between a mathematically inclined approach to the issue of Space and an ontological, or metaphysical one. It seems to me that in the former there has been, in the direction which so many of the arguments have taken, a disparaging, and ultimately a forsaking, of the realities of creation as the ground of knowledge, and, correspondingly, a disparaging and ultimately a forsaking, of the reminder that our mental capacities and our terminology are limited by the created dimension.

It further seems to me that we have to return from our theoretical wanderings and start afresh and champion finitude. That is our home. From a respectful appreciation of that great household of creation, we will find that its immensity and magnitude are more than enough to occupy our minds, and will, from the integrity of the created verities of which it is the totality, provide sufficient pointers to that which lies 'beyond' it. If the words 'infinite' and 'eternal' are to be used, these should be perceived to be comments on the limitations of our minds, rather than realities which we have discovered by rising out of our place and bursting the bounds of that condition by which we live and move and have our being.

If I have criticized philosophers for this, that is not to be taken as a dismissal of philosophy. But there is a boundary which even philosophy should acknowledge. The same criticism is applicable to theology. Too often what is called 'mysticism' and 'spirituality', and more especially that which is manifest in what are claimed to be movements of the Holy Spirit, have forsaken common sense, in the literal meaning of that phrase, and taken flight to regions unknown from God's good handiwork here 'below'.

Again, all too often, such attitudes and attempts are substitutes for honest theological discipline, ground work and debate – short cuts to supposed fulfilment of being. The accompanying tendency seen in some of these quarters is a spiritual arrogance and the growth of a subtle neo-gnosticism expressed in superior grouping of the initiated. At least philosophy does not experience this phenomenon, or overtly so at any rate.

Space, in terms of creation, I have suggested further, is not other than the 'room' which is the expression of an existence. This is not a type of Aristotelian thought, for this was a static concept, space being the bounds of a particular entity. The 'room' which I am seeking to describe is that existence both as it is in itself and as it is in relation to the integrity of other existences. It is not a void, infinite or otherwise, into which existences are fitted. It is the dynamic 'place' whereby any existence expresses itself and finds its relations with other existences, where one order of being opens out and interacts with another.

The whole space of the universe, as it expands, is not a question of the universe finding room in a vast container, again either infinite or finite. It is a matter of the expansion of the universe making space as it does so, or, theologically put, God permitting it to 'make room' for such is its nature as it is created by him. As to the question of what lies beyond space, the answer to that is simply 'nothing' – but not 'nothing' in the sense of a void or a vacuum. This 'nothing' is not even a concept; it is the final judgment on our conceptual limitations. It is 'beyond' concept and is the ultimate denial of all such, the verdict against which there is no createdly rational appeal.

When we assert the Christian doctrine of *creatio ex nihilo*, *creation out of nothing*, we must take this nothing seriously and utterly radically as that which lies beyond all perception and description because it lies 'beyond' all created being. It is not within our competence to apprehend how things came into being, for, as we are not the Creator but that which is created in company with all the rest of the universe, we cannot claim the prerogative of his way of working. This indeed is a case of *My thoughts are not your thoughts, neither are your ways my ways, saith the Lord*[2]. That the mode of creation is God decreeing that something should come out of nothing is beyond mortal ken.

This should bring us up short and stifle any abstractions about infinity with regard to the created order, and, conversely, it should throw us back to a consideration of creation as it is in itself. In that appreciation of its nature as created and therefore bounded, no matter how far its macroscopic immensities baffle our minds and its microscopic mysteries throw out their respective challenge, a consideration of its contingency to and from an Existence which radically is different from its existence precisely as creation will be forced upon us. The necessity of considering that Existence which has given it existence and on which it is doubly contingent can only lead to pondering an Existence utterly beyond our discovery and explanation. That is the only and true Infinite and Eternal, over against all concepts abstracted from what we already know and how we already think and which we describe as infinity and timelessness.

The profundity of the doctrine of the incarnation is that this Infinite and Eternal, the Author of all that is created and on whom all creation depends, without forsaking, changing, compromising, diluting or denying what he is in himself, takes our being and integrates it to his Existence. This is not a quantitative union between a greater and a lesser, whereby the greater swallows up the lesser and the lesser is lost in its essential being and nature in the greater. It is a union of two existences utterly distinct in their respective qualities.

It is on this qualitative distinction and union, whereby the Creator of all 'makes room' for his creation in his own Being, that the doctrine of recapitulation, the summing up of all things in that union of the Creator Word made flesh, depends.

I have sought to argue that such is the distinction between Infinity and Eternity and space and time, in the qualitative sense, that incarnation and creation are together the one act of that Infinite and Eternal God, incarnation being the mode of creation. For such is the relation to creation of that which is qualitatively different as Creator, that what we perceive as the created dimension of space and time is 'present' in its entirety in that creative act.

This, to my mind at least, does not dilute the seriousness of what we call 'evil', the shadow and the pain which characterise so much of our existence, movement and life and all that we see in the circumstances of the created order. Rather it heightens it as the created order's groaning and travailing as it participates in the cost which God has borne in creating an entity distinct from himself, which cost is expressed in the realities of our refracted existence in the incarnation and crucifixion of our Lord. There God's 'time' for us is manifest in our time, and his 'making room' for us in his creative decree takes our space to himself.

Here in incarnation and crucifixion the refractions of our created existence, which form the nature of creation expressed in time and space, are gathered up by the Being of the Creator sharing the frailty of his creation and making himself vulnerable to its vulnerability. In resurrection and ascension he anchors them beyond themselves in the Being of the Creator as their fulfilment, just as the refractions of light are gathered into a single beam. The Word made flesh is the commitment of God to his creation. But this cannot be a divine after-thought. Rather, such is his Existence as other than the existence of what he creates, it is the mode of his act of creation, wherein the end is joined to the beginning, the Alpha is also the Omega, in its refracted form in the dimension of our realities, but in which all things and all time are dynamically 'present' to him at creation.

I would suggest, for a matter of debate, since conclusions on such matters would be presumptuous to say the least, that the problem is twofold. First, if we make any distinction between incarnation and creation and see them other than the one act of God, we project, however unintentionally, a time lapse into God, thereby making him contingent upon time and the unwitting prisoner of what he has created.

It may well be argued that the bible informs us that God has done just that, or something like it, in the act of creation and in the abject spectacle of his Son crucified, and that unless we appreciate this we are in danger of diluting the acknowledgement of the existence and ravages of evil. My suggestion is that the biblical witness is set out in temporal/ spatial language, and points beyond what that literally conveys to the triumph of God in creating through incarnation.

This in fact would heighten the question of evil, for it places it firmly within the awareness of God as to what nature of entity, its frailty and vulnerability, he was creating. He takes the whole cost of this to himself, seriously, in creating through the mode of incarnation. Evil is then seen in all the terribleness of the full extent of its cosmic threat, and the creature's total need for maintenance against that threat of nothingness and all its temporal/spatial manifestations, from its foundations to its fulfilment.

It seems to me that any projection of time into God whereby creation and incarnation, from the side of God, are separated, raises absurd questions about God's omniscience and, indeed, love and grace. Is there a time when he leaves creation to its own devices in that his being is not fully involved with what he has created? Where then is the love and care of God? Is it that he is ignorant of what he has done in bringing this creation into being? Where then is his omniscience?

In so looking at the question from our side of creation, we indulge in the three-dimensional absurdity of unthinkingly casting doubt on the competence of God.

Second, questions of space arise, for, time and space being inseparable, the Being of God is separated from his gathering up the being of creation by time. If beings are separated by time, they are qualitatively no different; they exist on the same dimension. If there is a disjunction of time between creation and incarnation for the Being of God, then God can only be related to creation in a spatial way, for he can be of no qualitative difference from what the creature is and how it exists.

But if we say that all time is recapitulate as a dynamic present, where future and past are gathered up into that present in a way which is beyond what we call our 'present', with all the elusiveness and challenge to definition that that 'present' of our time has, then we are bound to say that space is involved too for temporal beings, or beings characterised by time, can only exist as spatial creatures.

This inseparability of space and time is a fact of this creation. This was recognized by Einstein's tutor, H. Minkowsky, who sowed the seed of all that has opened out in our awareness of the nature of the universe, through Einstein's work and its development since his day. Minkowsky wrote:

> The views of space by itself and time by itself which I wish to lay before you, have sprung from the soil of experimental physics, and therein lies their strength. They are radical. Henceforth, space by itself and time by itself are doomed to fade away into mere shadows, and only a union of the two will preserve an independent reality.

There has been much written in the field of physics and astrophysics developing this conclusion about the inseparability of time and space. For our purposes here, it poses the question to which we are driven if we project time into God, for then we are forced into perceiving God as having a spatial nature and existence. The conclusion of that is that we sink into a whole mythological slough, or a literalistic swamp, of absurdities.

Let us try to illustrate at least part of the problem of space and time as they appear to us. E. F. Taylor and A. J. Wheeler[3] set out in part of their book *Spacetime Physics* the example of John standing at his laboratory door. A rocket, carrying Mary, flashes past him, down the corridor and out the back door of the laboratory. An antenna projects from the rocket which is one millimetre away from a pen in John's pocket. As the rocket passes him, a spark jumps across from the antenna to the pen. The time of that event is recorded accurately by both John and Mary.

The rocket passes down the corridor and another spark jumps from the antenna to a fire extinguisher two metres down the corridor on the wall – the gap between antenna and fire extinguisher also being one millimetre. The time of that event is recorded by both observers, both using the time of the antenna/pen spark as their starting point and reference.

For Mary, both sparks occur in the same place – the end of her antenna. For John, two places are involved, separated by two metres. For Mary, the time between the sparks is one measurement; for John, another and slightly longer one.

Clearly, the result is a matter of the relativity of both observers and their state of motion to the events recorded. But here there has to be considered the speed of light, that is, the time that light takes from the moment of the spark between the antenna and the fire extinguisher to reach John at the place of the antenna/pen spark. The speed of light is the sole natural constant which can be used to convert time into length. It has to be recognized that it is a conversion factor which is necessarily employed because of the arbitrary choice by the human mentality of measuring distance, that is space, and time, as different units.

We may think of the fact that just as some of us may measure distance by metres and some by miles, or some employ metric values for weight and some imperial, so a conversion factor is required if we want to express to each other the same actuality of distance or the same value of weight.

What comes into play here in such problems of the relation between space and time, is the Einstein-Poincare discovery of *the invariant spacetime interval*, formally known as the Lorentz interval. In this, the speed of light is the conversion factor. The different times of the two sparks for both observers are multiplied by the speed of light to convert the seconds which elapse between the two events (in this case minute fractions of seconds expressed as *nanoseconds*) to convert them to metres. We now have a spacetime interval. The square of John's spacetime interval is then calculated by subtracting the square of the space separation from the square of the time separation. The same is done for Mary's calculations, and it is found that the same value of spacetime interval emerges for both John and Mary, despite the fact that both space and time separations of the sparks were different for them.

This invariant spacetime interval, being independent of all the observers of any event in whatever state of motion they may be (Mary's state of motion is different from John's) brings to our realization the fact that time and space, though they have different qualities, are inseparable and are parts of a single entity.

This may seem rather far from the question of God and his relation to the temporal/spatial creation. But it is significant for this issue. In the first place, if we ascribe time to God – that is for example, if God waits between his act of creation and his act of incarnation, and this waiting is an experience of his existence, then we must also project space into God, and this leads to absurdities. In fact the projection of time is as abhorrent as the projection of space. The only reason we merrily and unthinkingly project time into God is that time is somewhat nebulous as a concept in our estimation of it, while space expresses itself physically in visible measure of distances between objects.

Second, if we are relative to events within spacetime, then the totality of all our relativities is relative to God who is 'beyond', or qualitatively different from, space and time, and the whole spacetime creation is as a single entity and event to him, time and space being 'immediate' to his Existence as Creator, from its beginning to its end. His 'position' and 'vantage point' is that of the Creator of all, which is different from our vantage point and position as we observe and experience the things and events of creation from within it. We may ponder that the 'events' of creation and incarnation are separate for us in our refracted existence of time and space, but are as one for God in his 'vantage point'. That is why it is absurd for us to project time and space values, as we perceive them, into God's Existence.

God comprehends and holds to himself all space and time, not because he is quantitatively bigger, but because he is qualitatively different. That, I emphasize again, is the profundity of the incarnation, both because it is the taking into itself by that quality, which is other than space or time, the created realities qualified as a spatial/temporal reality, to itself as the source and sustainer and fulfiller of all things created, and also because it is the mode whereby God declares his total faithfulness to that which he has created, involving his very Being in that pledge.

That Being of God, committed to creation in His Word made flesh, expresses itself to us and to all creation by the Holy Spirit. The Spirit is the Bond which binds Creator and creation in their respective integrities. He is this Bond because of what he is in the inner life of the Trinity. God exists as Father and Son bound in the *Vincula Caritatis, the Bond of Love*, the Holy Spirit. This is the inner relation of the Holy Spirit within the Godhead. This the Christian faith believes on the basis of the Self-revelation of God, that is, not the knowledge of an object, but that knowledge which is a sharing in the knowledge which God has of himself, the Son knowing the Father and the Father the Son, in the Holy Spirit.

> ... God cannot be known without God: but that this is the express will of the Father, that God should be known. For they do know Him to whomsoever the Son has revealed him[4].
> ... the Son, administering all things for the Father, works from the beginning even to the end, and without Him no man can attain the knowledge of God. For the Son is the knowledge of the Father; but the knowledge of the Son is in the Father, and has been revealed through the Son; and this was the reason why the Lord declared: 'no man knoweth the Son, but the Father; nor the Father, save the Son, and those to whomsoever the Son shall reveal [Him]'[5].

The early Church perceived that the giving of the Holy Spirit was the prerogative of Christ as God and man – he being both the God who gives and the man who receives on behalf of all humanity and all creation. The Spirit is firmly anchored in, and mediated through, the incarnate Word, in the relation which that Word has to all creation. The Word, in assuming our humanity, opens that humanity out to the divine life which is his in his union with the Father in the Holy Spirit, giving it, in his assumption of it, that capability.

The Spirit comes from the inner life of the Trinity and from that inner life where the humanity which the Word assumed is 'given room' in the existence of the Triune God. It is the role of the Holy Spirit to bind us to that humanity within the life of the Trinity and to the fulfilment of all creation which that incarnate Word has accomplished.

The Spirit is the plenipotentiary agent of the Word and the Father, bringing the existence of all creation into relation with the Triune existence where that temporal/spatial existence has its fulfilment. It is worth quoting in full an example of the early church's belief in the matter. While I do not wish here to give an extended interpretation of the doctrine of the Holy Spirit, I do wish to emphasise several factors within that doctrine which concern creation and its 'space'. These are implicit in the following quotation from Irenaeus, the substance of which was later elaborated by Athanasius (of whom, I would say, Irenaeus was the hinge if Athanasius be the door of the Nicene faith, for the direction Athanasius takes in opening out so many profound issues, is found clearly in anticipation in Irenaeus), and the other 4th century Nicene fathers. For not only Athanasius is foreshadowed in so many of Irenaeus's dicta, but, for example, Basil's *De Spiritu Sancto*, to give his treatise its western appellation, is embryonic in Irenaeus's observations on the Holy Spirit. It is because of the way in which it embraces all the issues concerning this with precision and conciseness that I use the following[6]:

> For it is necessary that things that are made should have the beginning of their making from some great cause; and the beginning of all things is God. For He Himself was not made by any, and by Him all things were made. And therefore it is

right first of all to believe that there is One God, the Father, who made and fashioned all things, and made what was not that it should be, and who, containing all things, alone is uncontained[7]. Now among all things is this world of ours, and in the world is man: so then this world was also formed by God.

Thus then there is shown forth One God, the Father, not made, invisible, creator of all things; above whom there is no other God, and after whom there is no other God. And, since God is rational, therefore by (the) Word He created the things that were made; and God is Spirit, and by (the) Spirit He adorned all things: as also the prophet says: By the word of the Lord were the heavens established, and by His spirit all their power. Since then the Word establishes, that is to say, gives body and grants the reality of being, and the Spirit gives order and form to the diversity of powers; rightly and fittingly is the Word called the Son, and the Spirit the Wisdom of God. Well also does Paul His Apostle say: One God, the Father, who is over all and through all and in us all. For over all is the Father; and through all is the Son, for through Him all things were made by the Father: and in us all is the Spirit, who cries Abba Father, and fashions man into the likeness of God. Now the Spirit shows forth the Word, and therefore the prophets announced the Son of God; and the Word utters the Spirit, and therefore is Himself the announcer of the prophets, and leads and draws man to the Father.

This then is the order of the rule of our faith, and the foundation of the building, and the stability of our conversation: God, the Father, not made, not material, invisible: this is the first point [lit. bond] of our faith. The second point is: the Word of God, Son of God, Christ Jesus our Lord, who was manifested to the prophets according to the form of their prophesying and according to the method of the dispensation of the Father, through whom all things were made; who also at the end of the times, to complete and gather up all things, was made man among men, visible and tangible, in order to abolish death and show forth life and produce a community of union between God and man. And the third point is: The Holy Spirit, through whom the prophets prophesied, and the fathers learned the things of God, and the righteous were led forth into the way of righteousness; and who in the end of the times was poured out in a new way upon mankind in all the earth, renewing man unto God.

And for this reason the baptism of our regeneration proceeds through these three points: God the Father bestowing on us regeneration through His Son by the Holy Spirit. For as many as carry the Spirit of God are led to the Word, that is to the Son; and the Son brings them to the Father; and the Father causes them to possess incorruption. Without the Spirit it is not possible to behold the Word of God, not without the Son can any draw near to the Father: for the knowledge of the Father is the Son, and the knowledge of the Son of God is through the Holy Spirit: and, according to the good pleasure of the Father, the Son ministers and dispenses the Spirit to whomsoever the Father wills and as He wills.

And by the Spirit the Father is called Most High and Almighty and Lord of Hosts; that we may learn concerning God that He it is who is creator of heaven and earth and all the world, and maker of angels and men, and Lord of all, through whom all things exist and by whom all things are sustained; merciful, compassionate and very tender, good, just, the God of all ...

The factors I wish to emphasise from the above quotation, may be set out broadly. Again, these have all been taken up, particularly by the Nicene Fathers, and expanded. But we may note them here in their Irenaean context for their concentrated expression.

The work of creation is a work of the whole Trinity, the Father creating by the Son through the Spirit. Irenaeus delights to call the Word and the Spirit *the hands of God* [8]. The Father creates by his Word who establishes and consolidates being, while the Spirit disposes and gives order to creation. This is the one work of the one God.

The knowledge of God comes by the Spirit, who alone searches out the deep things of God [9]. Just as the spirit of a man only may know that man, so the Spirit of God only knows the profundity of the Being of God. It is on that Self-revelation alone that we have our starting-point in any thought about the Holy Spirit. We do not begin with what we perceive to be the manifestation of the Holy Spirit in his work towards creation – his work *ad extra*. Otherwise we remove the Holy Spirit from his proper existence in the mutual relations of the Trinity, as the Spirit of the knowledge which the Father has of the Son and the Son of the Father. We cannot know the Spirit by and of himself, as though he existed in isolation. We can know him only in his relation with the Father and the Word of both of whom he is that Bond of Love.

The Spirit has the same function *ad extra* – towards relation. As the outpoured Love of the Father through the Son, the Spirit binds the existence of creation to the existence of the Triune God. It is his role to take the things of the Word made flesh – all that Christ has accomplished – and give creation participation in that once and for all and sufficient work of Christ. This means that he upholds creation in reference to what it is in the Word. He illuminates with the light of the Light of Light, the Light of that Word of the Father, and enlightens with the same Light, sustaining creation as a creation of light and rationality, just as that Light created all things that exist in the power of that same Spirit.

The Spirit is always united to the Person and work of Christ. He does not speak of himself, and, if, as we have said already, the angels are self-effacing in their witness to the decrees and operations of God by his Word and through his Spirit, the Holy Spirit is supremely Self-effacing. He unveils and articulates the Word, so that the Word may be seen and heard as the Self-revelation of God.

But this is not just an imparting of knowledge. In that knowledge so given, the Spirit leads humanity to the Word who presents it to the Father. The Word to whom he leads is the Word made flesh wherewith is the recapitulation of all creation, and who, as such, has brought about a *community of union* of humanity with God. But humanity stands in relation to all creation, and the end of humanity's *community of union* with God is the embracing by God of all creation to his Divine Existence. It is to this that the Spirit leads humanity and therefore all creation, when that Spirit leads them to that Word.

The Spirit is seen by Irenaeus as he who binds the existence of creation to the Existence of God through the Word by whom all things were created. It is the Spirit who is concerned with the ordering of creation, the apportionment of 'place' for each existence. That is to say, the determination of the quality of each existence and its relation to and with other existences within the whole and to the whole, and therefore the 'place' each existence has and requires to its inter-relational nature within the whole, is the work of the Spirit. The determination of what we call 'space' – the totality of the living and lively relations of all 'places' of the universe – is the dynamic work and presence of the Holy Spirit, upholding, or *establishing*, or *ordering*, or *giving dispensation to* everything that exists, in his relation to the Word by whom all things were created.

It has to be noted that for Irenaeus, the *community of union* which is established by the Word through the Spirit concerns the relation of the whole creation with humanity at its heart, to God. This is no narrow 'spiritual' concept, confined to a solely ecclesiastical 'fellowship' with God. The role of the Church as the 'place' where this is known, is to call all humanity as the 'crown' of creation to this awareness of what it is in the Word by the Spirit.

The manifold 'gifts' of the Spirit, his distribution of the creation as the creation it is, and his distribution of 'places' within it, are seen to be the individual existences with their respective natures and qualities and capacities and actions. They are so seen and experienced, as we experience our own individual lives and existences from birth to death, and our relations with other individuals and existences within creation. We experience 'places' – perhaps literally places we have known or now know – parts of creation to which we particularly relate. In one sense they are very much a part of us, and we a part of them – our birth-place, for example. But these we experience within this refracted spatial/temporal dimension which is the sphere in which we live and move and have our being.

This whole spatial/temporal dimension, I would suggest, is already 'present' in its totality and fulfilment, in that one act of God in creating through the Word made flesh in the power of the Holy Spirit – the Hands of God embracing all time and things instantly, giving them their distinctive creaturely nature, and both safeguarding that nature and giving it its freedom to be what it is. All that we experience and all that we are here points to what we, and all things, 'already' are with Christ in God. So much of our experience is parabolic, pointing beyond to what we cannot yet perceive in its temporal/spatial immediacy – the immediacy of its resolution and fulfilment where the refracted light of our existence is gathered into that single beam of light in the 'Place' of God's Uncreated Light and affirmed and upheld by that Light.

Because all things are so relative to God in his Word and Spirit, the demise of each individual, our respective deaths, are the point where, in biblical terms *the trumpet shall sound, and the dead shall be raised incorruptible, and we shall be changed* [10], just as Christ's risen body was recognizable yet was not constrained by the constricts and limitations of refracted time and space, but, while not dissolving and dispensing with time and space, affirmed our temporal/spatial existence as that refraction gathered up in its fulness of existence as a dynamic present where past and future, beginning and end, are joined in the 'instant' creative act of God accomplished by incarnation.

The resurrection of the dead, the so-called 'Second Coming' (which is only to us one facet of the one 'Coming' of our Lord in the refracted dimension of our temporal/spatial existence), is that which is the fulfilment of our created existence and temporal/spatial dimension. Hence we are already raised with Christ; that is, we go to meet the One Who comes to meet us, the Alpha and Omega of all creation, the event where all created existence is confirmed in its real integrity, its refracted spacetime consummated as a dynamic present, the 'now' of its presence affirmed with Christ in God.

In the meantime we no doubt ponder many things about the refracted mystery of creation. We may look up to the heavens above and wonder at the immensity of it all. But we should not be sidetracked into trying to deal with it and explain it by our infinities and eternities. We make static and mechanical what God has made dynamic and lively. Rather, we should then avert our gaze and turn it to our own insignificance in the face of such an overwhelming spectacle. For in the recognition of that insignificance, we find ourselves in the company of the Word made flesh, by whom all things were made, for whom they were made, and in whom they consist, whom even the heaven of heavens cannot contain, but who in that 'Place' of God has prepared a 'place' for us – that perfection and fulfilment of all creation.

I find that the questions raised by the work of Edwin
Hubble in the 1920s, and the highlighting of them in all the
data from the Hubble telescope for scientists, are parallel to
those questions which have for so long intrigued theologians
dealing with the doctrine of creation. In the amazing expansion of the universe (and here one may think of the illustration of painting spots on a balloon, blowing it up and seeing
the spots, like galaxies, move uniformly away from each
other as the whole expands) there comes, pressing, the issue
that time and space are co-terminous with the universe, that
there was no time before the universe, no space outside it –
both come into existence with it. There is no 'where', no
'when', other than this created existence which, in its
dynamic nature shows that space and time can only be
thought of likewise dynamically but finitely, even if that finitude is more than our understanding. For the theologian this
can only mean the human mind's necessary awe and reverence called forth by creation, and thereby pointed to that
grace and love of God which has created, sustains and holds,
in an ineffable way by his Word, the totality of all that he has
made, things visible and invisible.

O Lord our Governor, how excellent is thy Name in all the
world: thou that hast set thy glory above the heavens!

Out of the mouth of very babes and sucklings has thou
ordained strength, because of thine enemies:
that thou mightest still the enemy and the avenger.

For I will consider thy heavens, even the works of thy fingers:
the moon and the stars, which thou hast ordained.

What is man, that thou art mindful of him:
and the Son of man, that thou visitest him?

Thou madest him lower than the angels:
to crown him with glory and worship.

Thou makest him to have dominion of the works of thy hands:
and thou hast put all things in subjection under his feet;

All sheep and oxen:
yea, and the beasts of the field;

The fowls of the air, and the fishes of the sea:
and whatsoever walketh through the paths of the seas.

O Lord our Governor:
how excellent is thy Name in all the world! [11]

Notes

Prologue
1. c.f. Aquinas: Summa Theologiae: Question LII, Articulus II: Questio LIII, Articulus II–III.
2. Not, he hastens to add, from any of the clergy of Worcester Cathedral!
3. M. F. Tupper (1810–1889): On Reading.
4. John Locke: Essay Concerning Human Understanding, Book II, Chapter XVII.
5. Hilaire Belloc: The Path to Rome, 1902.
6. Psalm VIII:I, 3–6, 9.
7. A. Einstein: Out of My Later Years, p. 33.
8. A. Einstein: The World as I See It, p. 18.

Chapter 1
1. Irenaeus; Demonstration of the Apostolic Preaching, 3.
2. Psalm 89:6 (AV).
3. Isaiah: 40:18.
4. Isaiah: 45:6.
5. Irenaeus: Adversus Haereses II:13:3, 4; c.f. II:13:8.
6. Athanasius: Discourses against the Arians I:3:57.
7. Irenaeus: Adversus Haereses III:16:3; c.f. Demonstration of the Apostolic Preaching 31, 47.
8. Basil: Hexaemeron I:7.
9. Athanasius: Contra Arianos II:21, 22: c.f. II:27, 31. 57ff.
10. Genesis I.
11. c.f. I. M. MacKenzie: The Anachronism of Time pp. 31–43.

Chapter 2
1. Gregory Nazianzen: Orations XXVIII:9; c.f. Athanasius: Ad Mon, 2; Basil: Con. Eun. I:10.
2. St John of Damascus, c750.
3. H. Bonar, 1803–1889.
4. Lancelot Andrewes: Sermon 15 of the Resurrection, Sermons 1635 edition, p. 548.
5. R. Grosseteste: Commentaries in VIII Libros Physicorum Aristotelis.
6. A. Einstein: Out of My Later Years, p. 33.
7. A. Einstein: The World as I See It, p. 18.

Chapter 3

1. R. Sorabji: Matter, Space and Motion: Theories in Antiquity and their Sequel, pp. 165ff.
2. Ibid, p. 168.
3. Aristotle: Physica, 3, 5, 206a, 27–29.
4. Sorabji: ibid, p. 169, citing Aristotle: Physica, 3, 6, 206a, 21–33, 30–33; 3, 7, 207b 14.
5. Aristotle: Physica 3, 6, 206b 33–207a 2.
6. Sorabji: ibid, p. 170.
7. Aristotle: Physica, 3, 6, 206a 14–23.
8. Aristotle: Physica, 3, 5, 204b 9; 6, 7, 238a, 33; An Post, 1, 3, 72b 11; Cael, 1, 5, 272a 3, etc.
9. Aristotle: Physica, 8, 8, 263b 5–6.
10. R. Sorabji: Matter, Space and Motion, p. 172.

Chapter 4

1. Philo: De Virtutibus 39:2:4.
2. c.f. Plato: Timaeus 28A: 29A: 52A.
3. c.f. Philo: e.g. De Opificio Mundi 6, 25.
4. c.f. Philo: De Post, Caini.
5. c.f. Philo: De Somn, 1:32:185.
6. Hermas: II: Commandment I (the Vatican and Palatine MSS add *and who cannot be defined in words, nor conceived by the mind* – so showing that 'contained' is not to be understood merely as 'explained').
7. c.f. Clement: Stromateis IV:25:156f; V:10:65; V:11:2.
8. c.f. Clement: Stromateis V:1–4.
9. c.f. Clement: Stromateis VII:2:6–7; Protrepticus I:4:7.
10. c.f. Clement: Stromateis VII:5:68f, VII:6.81.
11. Pseudo-Dionysius: The Divine Names 585B.
12. Pseudo-Dionysius: The Divine Names 589C.
13. Pseudo-Dionysius: The Divine Names 588C.
14. Pseudo-Dionysius: The Divine Names 648D–649A: c.f. The Celestial Hierarchy 181C.
15. Pseudo-Dionysius: The Mystical Theology 997Bff.
16. Pseudo-Dionysius: The Mystical Theology 1001A.
17. Pseudo-Dionysius: The Divine Names 588B.
18. Gregory Nazianzen: Orations XXX:17.
19. Gregory Nazianzen: Orations XXIX:8.
20. c.f. Gregory Nazianzen: The Fourth Theological Oration, the Second Concerning the Son, 17ff.
21. Gregory Nazianzen: Orations XXVIII:7.
22. Gregory Nazianzen: Orations XXVIII: 7–9.
23. Athanasius: Contra Arianos I:34, c.f. De Decr, 31.
24. Gregory Nazianzen: Orations XXVIII:11.
25. Gregory Nazianzen: Orations XXVIII:10.

Chapter 5

1. Gregory Nazianzen: Orations, XXVIII:9.
2. Athanasius: Contra Arianos I:9, 39, 558, 61; III:4, 6.
3. Athanasius: Contra Arianos III:15.
4. J. N. D. Kelly: The Athanasian Creed, A. and C. Black, 1964.
5. C. H. Turner's reconstruction of the Athanasian Creed from 7th-9th century MSS, cited in J. N. D. Kelly: The Athanasian Creed, pp. 17, 18.
6. Robert Grosseteste: Commentaries in VIII Libros Physicorum Aristotelis.
7. Athanasius: Contra Arianos, I:3:57.
8. Gregory Nazianzen: Orations XXVIII:9.
9. c.f. I. M. MacKenzie: The Anachronism of Time, The Canterbury Press, 1994, for a full discussion of this.
10. I. Corinthians, I:25, 27.
11. Hebrews: I:10–12, Psalm CII:25–27.
12. c.f. I. M. MacKenzie: The Anachronism of Time, passim.
13. James I:17.
14. K. Barth: Church Dogmatics, II:I, p. 463.
15. K. Barth: Church Dogmatics, II:I, p. 462.
16. Matthew Paris: Chronica Maiora, V, p. 404.
17. McEvoy: The Philosophy of Robert Grosseteste, pp. 6, 7.
18. Bulaeus: Historia Universitatis Parisiensis, III, pp. 154, 206, 709.
19. Aristotle: Physica 208b 1f; 209b 30f.
20. Aristotle: Physica 209a 31f.
21. Aristotle: Physica 209b 1f.
22. Athanasius: De Incarnatione Verbi Dei 17.
23. Gregory of Nyssa: The Great Catechism X, XI.
24. John of Damascus: Ekdos, 3. 7.

Chapter 6

1. Tertullian: On Monogamy V.
2. c.f. p. 40 above.
3. St John: I:2.
4. Ephesians: I:10.
5. Colossians: I:16, 17, 19.
6. B. Carter in: Confrontation of Cosmological Theories with Observation, ed. M.S. Longair, 1974.
7. Lancelot Andrewes: Sermons, 1635 edition; Sermon 7 on the Gunpowder Treason, pp. 958–970.
8. John Calvin: Institute of the Christian Religion I:I:2.
9. Psalm 36:9.
10. John Swan: Speculum Mundi, Hexameron, 1643 edition: 9:2, p. 489.

11. John Swan: Speculum Mundi, Hexameron, 1643 edition, 9:1, p. 488.
12. Irenaeus: Demonstration of the Apostolic Preaching, 1.
13. Irenaeus: Demonstration of the Apostolic Preaching, 3.
14. Irenaeus: Demonstration of the Apostolic Preaching, 2.
15. Irenaeus: Adversus Haereses IV:XVIII:5.
16. Athanasius: Contra Arianos: IV:6ff, c.f. ibid, I:41ff, 50ff, II:7ff, 12ff, 65ff, 74ff, III:30ff.
17. I. M. MacKenzie, The Anachronism of Time, c.f., e.g. pp. 147ff.
18. Gregory of Nyssa: Against Eunomius I:26.
19. Gregory of Nyssa: Against Eunomius I:26.
20. I. M. MacKenzie: The Anachronism of Time, pp. 44ff.
21. E.g. Athanasius: Contra Arianos II:18–43, 48; Expositio Fidei 1, 4.
22. E.g. Athanasius: Expositio Fidei 1, 4: Sermo Maior de Fide.
23. E.g. Irenaeus: Ad, Haereses III:18:7, IV:36:4, V:1:1–2, 15:3; Dem of the Apostolic Preaching 31, 34.
24. Gregory of Nyssa; On the Making of Man XVI:7ff.
25. R. Grosseteste: Commentaries in VIII Libros Physicorum Aristotelis.
26. Augustine: De Civitate Dei XII:18.
27. Irenaeus: Fragment VI.
28. Hilary of Poitiers: De Trinitate I:13.
29. Hilary of Poitiers: De Trinitate XII:37, 39.

Chapter 7
1. McEvoy: The Philosophy of Robert Grosseteste.
2. R. W. Southern: Robert Grosseteste: p. 136.
3. R. W. Southern: Robert Grosseteste, p. 137.
4. R. Grosseteste: Commentaries in VIII Libros Physicorum Aristotelis.
5. R. Grosseteste: Commentaries in VIII Libros Physicorum Aristotelis.
6. R. Grosseteste: Hexaemeron: II:X:4, Dales and Gieben p. 100.
7. c.f. I. M. MacKenzie: The Anachronism of Time pp. 80ff.
8. R. Grosseteste: Hexaemeron II:X:4; Dales and Gieben, p. 100.
9. R. Grosseteste: Hexaemeron VIII:IV:7.
10. R. Grosseteste: Dicta.
11. R. Grosseteste: De Cessatione Legalium III:ii:1.
12. Athanasius: Contra Arianos: II:2.
13. Romans: VIII:22.

Chapter 8
1. Gregory of Nyssa: Against Eunomius I:26.

2. Pseudo-Dionysius: The Mystical Theology, 1000B–1000C.
3. ed. A. M. Allchin: Landscapes of Glory: Daily Readings with Thomas Traherne: Darton, Longman and Todd, 1989.
4. Romans VIII:22.
5. Calvin: Commentary on Romans.
6. Karl Barth: Commentary on the Epistle to the Romans, pp. 302ff.
7. Karl Barth: Commentary on the Epistle to the Romans, p. 236.
8. Karl Barth: Commentary on the Epistle to the Romans, pp. 317f.
9. Karl Barth: Commentary on the Epistle to the Romans, pp. 311f.
10. Colossians I:16, 17.
11. Ephesians I:10.

Chapter 9
1. Colossians III:3.
2. Acts I:9.
3. Irenaeus: Adversus Haereses, III:19:6–8.
4. c.f. Genesis II:I; I Chronicles XVI:31; Psalm VIII:3, CXIII:4; Proverbs II:19; VIII:27, etc.
5. c.f. I Kings VIII:27; Psalm CXLVIII:4.
6. c.f. Psalm CIV:2; Isaiah XLIV:24.
7. c.f. Psalm CLXIV:5.
8. c.f. Isaiah XIII:13; Haggai II:6, 21.
9. c.f. Joel II:10.
10. c.f. Isaiah LXIV:1.
11. c.f. Isaiah XXXIV:4.
12. c.f. Jeremiah X:II.
13. I. Corinthians XV:40.
14. Philippians II:10.
15. Jeremiah IV:28.
16. Psalm XCVI:II; Isaiah XLIX:13; Revelation XII:12, etc.
17. Ephesians I:10.
18. Colossians I:16ff.
19. Genesis I:1.
20. Nehemiah IX:6.
21. c.f. I Kings VIII: 27; Job XI:8; Psalm VIII:1; LVII:5 CXIII:4, etc.
22. Ephesians IV:10.
23. Romans VIII:39.
24. Colossians I:15ff.
25. E.g. Isaiah LXIII:15.
26. c.f. Psalm II:4; CIII:19; Ezekiel X:1; Isaiah LXVI:1, etc.
27. Ephesians I:20, 21.

28. Hebrews II:16.
29. Hebrews I:14.
30. St John III:13.
31. Genesis XXVIII:17.
32. Karl Barth: Church Dogmatics III:3; p. 459; c.f. Pseudo-Dionysius: The Celestial Hierarchy 200C ff and The Ecclesiastical Hierarchy 372C.
33. K. Rahner: Sacramentum Mundi, Vol. 5, p. 333.

Chapter 10
1. Karl Barth: Church Dogmatics III:3, pp. 369ff.
2. Origen: De Principiis I pref.
3. Gregory Nazianzen: Orations XXVIII:31.
4. Karl Barth: Church Dogmatics III:3, p. 371.
5. Karl Barth: Church Dogmatics III:3, pp. 376–377.
6. Augustine: Ep. 187, 11.
7. R. Grosseteste: Sacerdotes tui induantur iustitiam: Charge delivered to the clergy on the imitation of angelic contemplation and action, possibly when he was Archdeacon of Leicester.
8. R. Grosseteste: Hexaemeron II:VIII:1ff.
9. R. Grosseteste: Hexaemeron II:IV–IX.
10. c.f. Augustine: De Civitate Dei XI:6–9.
11. Augustine: De Civitate Dei XI:9.
12. Augustine: De Civitate Dei XI:6.
13. R. Grosseteste: Hexaemeron II:vii:1.
14. R. Grosseteste: Hexaemeron II:vii:1, Dales and Gieben p. 94.
15. R. Grosseteste: Hexaemeron II:vii:1, Dales and Gieben, p. 95.
16. R. Grosseteste: Hexaemeron II:ii:1.

Epilogue
1. Lancelot Andrewes: Sermons, 1635 edition; Certaine Sermons Preached at Sundry Times, Upon Severall occasions, pp. 129ff.
2. Isaiah: LV:8.
3. E. F. Taylor and T. A. Wheeler: Spacetime Physics, W. H. Freeman and Co., New York, 1992.
4. Irenaeus: Adversus Haereses IV:6:5 (here I have followed the received text, in which 'know' is in the present, though Harvey reasons that it should be in the future – 'shall know' – presumably because the future is used in all following like references).
5. Irenaeus: Adversus Haereses IV:6:7.
6. Irenaeus: Demonstration of the Apostolic Preaching 4–8 (translated by J. Armitage Robinson).

7. This is a paraphrase of what Irenaeus quotes as Scripture in Adversus Haereses IV:24:2 – which is from The Shepherd of Hermas I.
8. E.g. Irenaeus: Demonstration of the Apostolic Preaching 11; Adversus Haereses IV:pref.3; IV:14:1; V:1:3; V:5:1; V:6:1; V:25:3.
9. c.f. I Corinthians II:10–11.
10. I Corinthians XV:52.
11. Psalm VIII.

Select Bibliography

Allchin, A. M.: *Landscapes of Glory: Daily Readings with Thomas Traherne*, Darton, Longman and Todd, 1989.

Andrewes, Lancelot: *XCVI Sermons*, 1635 edition.

Athanasius: *Select Works, A Select Library of Nicene and Post-Nicene Fathers*, 1891.

Augustine: *Select Works, A Select Library of Nicene and Post-Nicene Fathers*, 1886.

Barth, K: *Commentary on the Epistle to the Romans*, Oxford University Press, 1977; *Church Dogmatics*, vols. I: 1 & 2: II: 1 & 2; III: 1, 2, 3 & 4; IV: 1, 2 & 3, T. and T. Clark, 1956–1975.

Basil: *Select Works, A Select Library of Nicene and Post-Nicene Fathers*, 1894.

Calvin, J.: *Institutes of the Christian Religion*, trans. H. Beveridge, Eerdmans, 1979.

Edwards, P. (ed.): *The Encyclopaedia of Philosophy*, Macmillan, 1967.

Einstein, A., *Out of my Later Years*, The Philosophical Library, New York, 1950; *The World as I See It*, J. Lane, 1935.

Ehrhardt, A.: *The Beginning: A Study in the Greek Philosophical Approach to the Concept of Creation from Anaximander to St. John*, Manchester University Press, 1968.

Gregory of Nazianzen: *Select Works, A Select Library of Nicene and Post-Nicene Fathers*, 1893.

Gregory of Nyssa: *Select Works, A Select Library of Nicene and Post-Nicene Fathers*, 1892.

Grosseteste, R.: *De Cessatione Legalium*; *Hexaemeron*, text by Dales and Gieben, Oxford University Press for the British Academy; *Commentaries on VIII Libros Physicorum Aristotelis*; *De Luce*.

Irenaeus: *Select Works, The Ante-Nicene Fathers, Edinburgh edition*, 1884.

Kelly, J. N. D.: *Early Christian Doctrines*, A. & C. Black, 1980; *The Athanasian Creed*, A. & C. Black, 1964; *Early Christian Creeds*, Longmans, 1952.

McEnvoy, J.: *The Philosophy of Robert Grosseteste*, Clarendon Press, Oxford, 1986.

MacKenzie, I. M.: *The Anachronism of Time*, The Canterbury Press Norwich, 1994.

Moore, A. W.: *The Infinite*, Routledge, 1990.

Origen: *Select Works, The Ante-Nicene Fathers, Edinburgh edition*, 1885.

Prestige, G. L.: *God in Patristic Thought*, S.P.C.K., 1956.

Sorabji, R.: *Matter, Space and Motion: Theories in Antiquity and Their Sequel*, Duckworth, 1988.

Southern, R.: *Robert Grosseteste, The Growth of an English Mind in Mediaeval Europe*, Clarendon Press, Oxford, 1988.

Swan, J.: *Speculum Mundi or a Glasse Representing the Face of the World*, 1643 edition.

Torrance, T. F.: *Christian Theology and Scientific Culture*, Christian Journals, Belfast, 1980; *The Ground and Grammar of Theology*, Christian Journals, Belfast, 1980; *Theology in Reconciliation*, Geoffrey Chapman, 1975; *Theology in Reconstruction*, SCM Press, 1965; *God and Rationality*, Oxford University Press, 1971; *Space, Time and Incarnation*, Oxford University Press, 1969; *Space, Time and Resurrection*, The Handsel Press, 1976; *Theological Science*, Oxford University Press, 1978; *Transformation and Convergence in the Frame of Knowledge*, Christian Journals, Belfast, 1984; *Divine and Contingent Order*, Oxford University Press, 1981; *The Trinitarian Faith*, T. & T. Clark, 1988.

Wood, E.: *Whosoever Will: Quicunque Vult*, Faith Press, 1961.

Index